HAPPINESS

Your Route Map to Inner Joy

HAPPINESS

Your Route Map to Inner Joy

• • • • • •

ANDY COPE WITH
ANDY WHITTAKER AND
SHONETTE BASON-WOOD

First published in Great Britain in 2017 by Hodder & Stoughton.
An Hachette UK company.

This edition published in 2017 by John Murray Learning

British Library Cataloguing in Publication Data: a catalogue record for this title is available from the British Library.

Library of Congress Catalog Card Number: on file.

ISBN 978 1 47365 102 9

eISBN 978 1 47365 104 3

2

The publisher has used its best endeavours to ensure that any website addresses referred to in this book are correct and active at the time of going to press. However, the publisher and the author have no responsibility for the websites and can make no guarantee that a site will remain live or that the content will remain relevant, decent or appropriate.

The publisher has made every effort to mark as such all words which it believes to be trademarks. The publisher should also like to make it clear that the presence of a word in the book, whether marked or unmarked, in no way affects its legal status as a trademark.

Every reasonable effort has been made by the publisher to trace the copyright holders of material in this book. Any errors or omissions should be notified in writing to the publisher, who will endeavour to rectify the situation for any reprints and future editions.

This book is for information or educational purposes only and is not intended to act as a substitute for medical advice or treatment. Any person with a condition requiring medical attention should consult a qualified medical practitioner or suitable therapist.

Cover image © Amy Bradley

Typeset by Integra, India

Printed and bound in Great Britain by Clays Ltd, St Ives plc

John Murray Learning policy is to use papers that are natural, renewable and recyclable products and made from wood grown in sustainable forests. The logging and manufacturing processes are expected to conform to the environmental regulations of the country of origin.

Carmelite House
50 Victoria Embankment
London EC4Y 0DZ

www.hodder.co.uk

HELLO TO JASON ISAACS

CONTENTS

BEFORE THE OFF

Famously, Archimedes experienced his eureka moment in the bath, Colonel Sanders had his in a kitchen in Kentucky and J K Rowling had hers in a café in Edinburgh.

Less famously, I had mine just outside Swadlincote, in the pouring rain. *Writing a personal development book in the style of a travel guide!* Immediately, I liked it. My mind whirred with places we could visit, analogies to be had, not to mention the fun.

But everyone has doubts so it wasn't long before my mind turned to questions. I write kids' books for a living, so I figure my mental age of 8¾ isn't typical. Just because *I'm* excited, doesn't mean anyone else will be. Maybe a 'happiness travel book' isn't such a good idea? Nobody's done it before. Does that mean it's not worth doing, or that it's not actually possible?

The rain came down harder and Swadlincote was looking particularly bleak. What if instead of running naked down the street, Archimedes had just continued soaking in his bath? What if The Colonel had kept his secret chicken recipe to himself? What if JK had thought her idea about a boarding school for wizards was too stupid for words?

What if, out of a dozen years of PhD research, my 100,000-word thesis needed translating into something enlightening, informative and fun? And a travel guide was the perfect vehicle?

I decided it'd be worth giving it a really good go, especially if it enabled me to poke fun at academia, therapy, religion, society and myself. To paraphrase Stan from *South Park*, just because we laugh doesn't mean we don't care.

I hope you enjoy the journey.

15

Happiness Book

Travel Book

Andy c

Shonette

Andy w

welcome ABOARD!

Chapter 1
TRAVEL PLANNING

· · · · · · ·

In which we plan the route, whetting your appetite for the journey ahead.

We come clean right at the start (just so we don't get a bad review on TripAdvisor) that your journey is a circuitous one, similar to the Circle Line, with a combo of stellar and scary stops along the way. After a detour to the Wild West we turn you inside out and take a peek at your slimy innards. Then, joy upon joy, we reveal that we've brought thinking back where it always belonged – *inside* the effing box!

We teach you a smidgeon of German and Zulu, your tour guides are introduced by a couple of (deliberately) terrible jokes before we set off to the steamy jungles of Costa Rica where we learn our first happiness lesson.

If you're going to play the game and stick with our travel analogy, then you'll be needing one special item for your suitcase and *voila!*, happiness lesson #2 is revealed without you even realizing.

Welcome aboard.

......

SCHNAPSIDEE (GERMAN): 'AN INGENIOUS PLAN HATCHED WHILE DRUNK.'

......

Call off the Search

Welcome to your happiness travel guide, a book like no other, a colourful childlike romp through lots of exciting lands that need to be experienced on the road to happiness. Plus, there's more. It's not just about places – we're also taking you to different time zones and altitudes in an immersive experience of the full emotional spectrum.

But don't let the pictures fool you. This guide is not really for children; it comes with a 15 certificate, containing as it does descriptions of lives of mild terror with adult themes. Some of the journeys are very perilous indeed.

......

UBUNTU (ZULU): ROUGHLY TRANSLATES AS 'WHAT YOU LEAVE BEHIND IS NOT WHAT IS ENGRAVED ON STONE MONUMENTS, BUT WHAT IS WOVEN INTO THE LIVES OF OTHERS'.

......

Before we get going, let's kick off with a classic black and white cowboy movie, a time when men with pickaxes swarmed across Colorado, Arizona and California because 'there's gold in them thar hills'.

Yes, but they're very big hills and there's not much gold. Where do we start?

The guys then didn't have time to hang around, it was called a 'gold rush' for a reason. They were prospectors which meant they made an educated guess, toiling in the heat, panning the river beds or hacking the rocks, searching for the elusive glint of something valuable.

Most toiled their entire lives without ever striking lucky.

Cut to today and the toil continues. It's less about gold (although we do toil for a salary which enables us to buy sparkly things) but the sweat is just the same. We're panning for happiness, looking everywhere. As was the case with cowboys, 'everywhere' is massive, so where should we start?

It used to bug me when I read books that said 'happiness is within'. I felt it was some sort of philosophical cop-out. Dear guru, I know you mean well but I don't want answers *within* – I want you to tell me where I can find it *out there*!

It took quite a few years of reading and research until I started to see that the Wild West metaphor was the proper answer. Indeed, the only answer. Finally, I could stop wielding my metaphorical pickaxe and mop my brow. The search was over. I was already at 'happiness'. In fact, I'd always been there, I'd just forgotten where and how to look.

We think that 'happiness' is basically an incredibly simple subject and, deep down, we all know how to be happier. In fact, if I asked the question, 'Could you be happier even if nothing in the world around you changed?', your probable answer would be (after you've spun it around in your head to work out if it's a trick question and realized it isn't), a rock solid 'yes'.

So, hang on a second – you could be happier. Nothing needs to change around you. So why aren't you? That simple question sends us down Alice in Wonderland's rabbit warren of confusion and 'six impossible things before breakfast'. Why aren't you happier? It seems the only thing really stopping you is you. Of course, we can fiddle around the edges of your happiness. You could change things 'out there' – your house or your partner, perhaps? Or you could demand a pay rise? Your new house, partner and income might improve your happiness? There's also a fair-to-middling chance that they won't. Besides, none of them are doable, today. Now. The only things you can change RIGHT NOW are things within. So what is this 'within' thing? If we turned you inside out and had a good look, you'd be full of slimy pink and purple stuff, some bones, a few miles of intestines and seven pints of blood. All a bit of a mess to be honest. The more interesting stuff that lies 'within' is less visible but can be of equal messiness. Your thoughts, memories and attention. Your spirit, beliefs and attitudes. These are the things that you have instant control over and these are the keys to flourishing.

If you roll these into just a couple of biggies, we'd dare to suggest that your thoughts and consciousness are where happiness resides. This leads us to some whopping questions such as what are thoughts and where do they come from? Who taught us how to think (and who taught them)? Plus, what the heck is 'consciousness' anyway?

We don't want to give you a pounding headache. In fact, quite the opposite. We want to unravel some of these heavy questions, but in a way that doesn't seem heavy. There is a massive amount of our collective livor poured into this book, alongside a significant chunk of academic underpinning. The aim is, of course, to make it look as if that's not the case.

Thank you for choosing our book. Our fingers and toes are tightly crossed.

Your Tour Guides

Before we set off, let's glimpse behind the scenes of the murky world of publishing. Before you write a book, you have to, for obvious reasons, prove there's a market for it. Publishers have various ways of going about it but this generally involves the author filling in a lengthy questionnaire where one of the questions is 'who will read this book?'

Our first very innocent response to this was 'everyone' because 'everyone' wants to be happier, right? We've all got room to turn our happiness dial up a notch, maybe even two notches? But then we had a rethink. While it's true that 'everyone' wants to be a tad happier, not everyone will like our style. So we thought, how can we narrow it down very early on, so that this book doesn't end up in the wrong hands?

It's a funny thing, humour. Brace yourself for a couple of fruit-based gags – I'm writing them for a reason, I promise.

Joke number 1: *If a doctor eats an apple a day does she have an existential crisis?*

Now, this isn't an exact science but we reckon that if you understand that joke, you'll probably not enjoy this book. The gag is too academic and if you chuckled, you're way too clever. Go and choose a book with more words and fewer pictures. In fact, no pictures.

Joke number 2: *I spy with my little eye, something beginning with D.*

Banana? (dyslexic I spy)

If you preferred this joke then you should stick with our book. This second joke is much funnier and just a little bit wrong. While the main purpose of this book is not to have you belly-laughing from start to finish, we do want to amuse and in the same way that dyslexic people who've had a humour by-pass might find the banana joke offensive, we might occasionally push the wrong buttons.

Next up, we have to get into the heads of our potential readership and make certain assumptions as to what style you might prefer. Crikey, that's a difficult call, but here goes – we've made the bold assumption that you want something different, so no bullshit, psychobabble or patronizing clichéd nonsense? We're hazarding that you're living a pressured life and are honoured that you've even considered reading our book, never mind actually getting this far. We're guessing that you're not ever-so keen on being asked to do 'blue-sky thinking' or to 'think outside the box', so we've decided to go retro and bring thinking back where it belongs, firmly inside the box. You'll already have noticed a couple, but basically it means you'll get bits and pieces like this ...

> 'We cannot have a meaningful revolution without humour.'
>
> *Bell Hooks*

Yes. Juicy tit-bits of our favourite quotes or pithy translations (to help you on your travels), distilled down to the basics, delivered (retro-style and reassuringly) *inside* the box.

And so to one last question, a rather terrifying biggy: why listen to us? *Come on, self-appointed tour guides, what qualifies you to write a book about happiness?*

For a start, you couldn't get three more different characters. That can be a recipe for either chaos or awesomeness – I guess the Amazon reviews will be the judge of that. We've all arrived at 'happiness central' via different routes but the point is that we have got there, eventually. Now here's a technical but important point, rather than switching between authors we're going to let Andy C do the talking. He's got a PhD in Happiness which trumps Andy W's GCSE

Woodwork (grade D, School of Hard Knocks) and Shonette's Diploma in Magic Wand Therapy (level 3, distinction, Waltons' Mountain Academy).

So we're your tour guides and, as you'll see, happiness depends not one jot on your qualifications. We have a range of happiness backgrounds but are speaking as one. Imagine us waving our brollies for your attention ... *Booked for the happiness tour? Ready? We've got a lot of ground to cover so let's crack on...first stop, Central America ...*

Lonely Planet

A couple of years ago my family and I went on holiday to Central America. Costa Rica intrigued me because it rained every day, they are much poorer than the Brits and, amazingly, they are the only country in the world that doesn't have an army. Imagine, no army? What kind of message does that send out to potential invaders? *We have an open door policy. Please wipe your feet on the way in. Put your Kalashnikov in the umbrella stand, sit yourselves down and let's have a coffee and a chat.* Costa Rica also happened to top the world happiness league tables so off we went and had the best fact-finding fortnight ever.

One day, we were trekking through the steamy jungle, looking for wildlife. The books said it would be teeming with weird creepy crawlies, armadillos, monkeys, exotic birds and those cute little green tree-frogs that adorned the cover of our Lonely Planet guide. I led the way, intrepid explorer style, aware that they also have leopards. Please note, this was proper dense Costa Rican rainforest, not British woodland. Imagine dark, steamy, creepy and you won't be far off. There were four of us, treading carefully, examining trees, undergrowth, rocks ... nothing except a few Chernobyl sized ants. That's four pairs of eyes, looking very hard. After an hour of trekking and seeing absolutely nothing, we came across a ranger, basically a local guy who does jungle tours. In my broken Spanish I jabbed at my tree-frogged guidebook and grumbled about the lack of tropical beasties: 'Where are the creatures? Are they having a day off?'

'Que?' He looked a little confused. The ranger approached the nearest tree and picked at one of the branches. It was a stick insect.

He bent into a bush and plucked out an iconic green tree-frog – 'OMG, that's the one off the book cover,' exclaimed my daughter.

He reached up and pointed to a toucan. He rattled a tree and the monkeys scattered, shrieking through the branches. He bent down and picked up the most humungous beetle any of us have ever seen and my family were agog as he let it crawl across my hand.

Let's make this abundantly clear. You've picked this book up for a reason. And it's quite a sturdy little number, published by a proper publisher. We're crediting you with enough intelligence to *get* the tree-frog story. It's no good having your eyes wide open if your mind is half-closed.

Happiness is one of those things that is so obvious it's hidden in plain sight and, no, the road to happiness doesn't actually go anywhere but we'll show you where and how to look so that you can truly enjoy the journey.

We are incredibly proud and excited to be your tour guides.

As Del Boy would say, 'bon appetite' x

Cool travel quote

'You're off to Great Places! Today is your day! Your mountain is waiting, So... get on your way!'

'Oh, The Places You'll Go!'

Dr Seuss

Top Tip

We're going to end each chapter with some happiness top tips. Normally, they'll follow logically from the content of each chapter and will take the form of a series of bullet points. But, for this chapter, in line with helping you pack for the trip of a lifetime, there's just one tip, in fact, more of a favour ...

Pop upstairs to your bedroom and open your underwear drawer. In that drawer will be some pants that you don't really fancy. You know the ones, your 'last resort knickers'? They have been in there a long time and have maybe gone from white to grey. Or you bought a three-pack of pants that have never been quite right but they're still in there: emergency knickers, for a very grey day. I want you to identify said knickers and remove them. Then bin them, burn them or bury them in your garden so you never have to wear them again.

Because tomorrow, when you're showered, deodoranted and are getting dressed for work, you will open your underwear drawer and in there will be your 'special knickers'. Once again, you know exactly which ones I mean. And I want you to wear your special knickers for work tomorrow. That means when you pull up in the car park and stroll in to work you will have a certain sparkle and *je ne sais quoi* because you know what's cracking off down below. Please note, this is not some sort of crass sexual laugh, there is a bit more science behind my special pants top tip than meets the eye. The sad fact is that on Monday morning most people's aim is to get through the week or survive until their next holiday – wishing their weeks away and placing happiness as a dot on the horizon. Similarly, we tend to save our 'special pants' for a special occasion.

Here's a focusing fact: the average life-span is 4000 weeks. Life is indeed a very short and precious gift. So our 'special pants' top tip is simply to quit waiting. Life is the ultimate special occasion.

Chapter 2
ZOMBIE LAND

●●●●●●

In which we start with death before gradually coming alive.

Bruce Willis gets a mention before we delve into 'accelerated history', covering 17,000 years in two pages flat, and that's kind of the point of this chapter: fast and brief to the point of not quite being enough.

We introduce you to the three apocalyptic horsemen of modernity that give rise to an epidemic of grumbling. We make a very big point about 'emptiness' (in fact it's so big we make it three times) before finishing with happiness lessons from bedtime stories and all-you-can-eat breakfasts.

Welcome to Zombie Land. We're delighted you could join us. Before the off, a word of warning: please don't engage with the locals, they're infectious.

••••••

KAROSHI (JAPANESE): WORKING YOURSELF TO DEATH. LITERALLY.

••••••

Alive but not Living

Cotard delusion, or 'walking corpse syndrome', is a rare mental illness where the sufferer claims to be dead. It's very hard to imagine, but thinking you're dead must be a terrible life to be living. It brings me on to something less serious but far more insidious, the fact that too many people are having a near-life experience or what I'm calling 'Sixth Sense Syndrome'. In case you've not seen the movie *Sixth Sense* let me regale you with the very basics – it's a scary movie in which Bruce Willis tries to help a small boy overcome his nightmares. There's a particularly chilling scene where the teary-eyed lad tells Bruce Willis, 'I see dead people'.

In the movie, he literally can. And in everyday life, I metaphorically can. Okay, so they're not actually dead, but look around you on a winter's Monday morning and you'll see legions of people in a zombie-like trance, trudging to work. There's a pulse, but there's not much aliveness. So, in a world of abundance, with a smorgasbord of first-world choices laid out before us, how on earth did we arrive in Zombie Land?

If you're a proper historian (i.e. know Henry VIII's wives, in the right order, what became of each one and the correct century), skip on a couple pages. If you're a mere mortal (*there was an Anne, maybe two? And did he have a fling with Mother Theresa?*) strap yourself in, we're setting coordinates for the year 6021.

Not so long ago, your ancestors lived in a little house and had a field, a goat and some hens. I'm talking about the Middle Ages, where from the fifth to fifteenth centuries, almost nothing happened. Yes, yes, I know, there were famines and wars and the Black Death but the chances are that your relatives led a simple life that never extended beyond the boundaries of their village. The potential pool of suitors was very small. Early on they realized it was a bad idea if you married your sister so the choice was extended to cousins. Still not good, so relationships were extended as far as the next village. Everyone knew their place and life was a simple existence – humanity inched along with no running water, central heating, TV or Wi-Fi – carried out on a small flat earth, overseen by a god. Life was harsh but your ancestors were lucky because, by definition, they managed to pass on their genes. Apart from a few brief interludes of joy, the aim was not to suffer too much. The deal was they'd be guaranteed an eternity of happiness when they died. In fact, this 'guarantee' was what kept them in order and, more often than not, death was a bit of a relief from the relentless daily grind that was 'living'.

It had been like this almost forever and then, like a bunny from a hat, Copernicus conjured the idea that the earth wasn't the centre of the universe. We'd been sold a pup. Our planet was, in fact, rotating around the sun, not the other way around. *Circa* 1500, this was pretty big news. Then it got a whole lot worse when someone sailed to the edge of the horizon and didn't fall off the end.

Science continued to rumble along until it collided in a big bang with politics and philosophy in the 'long eighteenth century' (1685–1815), heralding an era known simply as The Enlightenment. This is when it all kicked off with a fracture of thinking, away from the age-old *You'd jolly well better believe what we tell you* towards Kant's summary statement of *Dare to know! Have courage to use your own reason!* Excuse my paraphrasing, but what The Enlightenment seemed to be saying is that we don't have to suffer any longer. We don't have to believe what the good book tells us. We don't have to wait until the afterlife to be happy. We can have free will to think for ourselves and work out a better way.

Jinkies, these were heady days. It was indeed a revolution of thought and we all know what happens when people are allowed to think for themselves ... cue a whole series of bloody revolutions, most notably in France and America, when lots of people lost their heads (literally and metaphorically).

Cut to semi-modern times. The ante was upped to fever-pitch when Mr Darwin came along with his new-fangled idea about evolution and the whole God thing wobbled a bit more. Then Arkwright invented factories and, hey presto, gave birth to the industrial revolution and mass rural–urban migration.

Britannia ruled the waves but her grip was loosening as the Empire began to strike back. A couple of big wars later and the Brits had lost their competitive advantage. Those pesky foreigners had twigged how to make stuff better and faster so we closed our mines and factories and looked to set the standard in services. That was only possible because of the internet morphing into a super-slick, ultra-quick, speeder-upper of everything.

Fast-forward to right now where the pace of everything has been ratcheted up and our institutions are struggling to cope. Schools, for example; sure they've changed, but not nearly as fast as the world around them. To use Jamie Smart's words: 'The Western world is hobbled by educational institutions, social structures and habitual ways of thinking developed for a bygone era of smokestacks, whistles and assembly-lines.'[1] Yes, 'change' has affected how we work but Jamie's quote also draws in the fabric of society.

In the background, physics gave us some hard-and-fast laws before morphing into its steroid-pumping alter-ego, quantum physics and, whoosh, we're bang up to date in a world where Stephen Hawking bamboozles us with his electronic voice about quarks, big bangs, singularity and the Copenhagen question (don't ask!) And, as I type, even 'string theory' is beginning to unravel, replaced by M-theory's 11th dimension.

Pausing for breath, my wider point of this gentle opening salvo is that we've gone from a staid and miserable existence where, for a thousand years, not much changed, to a modern world of chaotic abundance. I'm not arguing that change is bad. In fact, far from it – the modern workplace is more humane – but instead of slogging it out down the pit at the coalface we've become prisoners in a digital chain gang, hacking away at the typeface.

In 'change' terms, we've gone from 'inching along' to 0–100 in 0.03 seconds, eyes wide and cheeks wobbling as the g-force of modernity pins us down. The world has evolved much more rapidly than our brains, stuck as they are in hunter-gatherer mode (have you ever wondered why women wear leopard print knickers, and men love barbecues?).

In a very short space of time we've evolved from carnivores to infovores, gobbling data, Mr Creosote style, until we're beyond bloated. We're faster, but no happier, having evolved from 'staid and miserable' to 'rapid and miserable'.

In fact, a rather daring question is that we're living life fast, but are we living it well? Technology has solved old economic problems by giving us new psychological ones. Life is so pacey that we tend to skim the surface and we know there's more to it than that. Scratching the surface of reality, we find it's not, in fact, 'real'. We'll sow that seed and come back to it later, but following the ill-logic, if 'reality' isn't real, then neither is 'happiness' – as in, 'happiness' isn't a 'thing'. It hasn't got a shape, form or mass. It's not something that you can cart around in a wheelbarrow. Happiness, in line with all your other emotions, is a mental construct. It's an emotion and it can only ever come from one place – *your* thoughts. So in its purest sense, 'happiness' is only ever one thought away. And this is where the science of happiness gets murky – if it's the thing we desire most, and it's in our control, why the heck is it so damned elusive?

Modern life is, on the whole, fantastic. But in a big bang of oxymoronic juxtapositioned irony, the 21st century gives and impedes our happiness. Yes, just like the Lord, modernity doth giveth and taketh away.

I've already alluded to one of the horsemen of the modern apocalypse, 'busyness', a manifestation of the modern world that jousts us off our happiness horse. Here, for your delectation are the other apocalyptic riders, 'emptiness' and 'enoughness'.

Emptiness

Forget Capitalism, Socialism or Communism, there's a new type of social disorder in town: 'commotionism'; the background noise of life has become a deafening hullabaloo. When I go out for a coffee or lunch and my date puts their mobile on the table, I'm immediately on edge. What they're really saying is *Look here Andy, I know I've granted you 15 minutes for a coffee and a chat but I'm going to leave my phone here and if it buzzes, rings or lights up, I'll be on it in a flash. Because it's more important than you.* They don't actually say it, but that's what I'm hearing.

> **Parenting tip**
>
> *Find out which of your kids is at home by simply turning off the Wi-Fi.*

Brace yourself for something that might sound unkind. What if busyness is a ruse, a disguise we can wear to shield us from depth? Let me try again – I can't help thinking that we might be cramming loads of stuff in to disguise an inner-emptiness that manifests itself in that Monday morning feeling of minor glumness in the pit of your stomach. That nagging thought that, as your 4000 weeks flash by, *is this it?* ... Stimulation and media are like bubble gum – they keep you occupied but there is little nutritional value. You can lose a couple of hours scrolling through Facebook but believe me when I tell you, social media is not your purpose (in fact, I'm not telling, I'm pleading!). How many shared meals have been ruined by one of you picking up emails or receiving a call? How many evenings have you wasted watching reality TV? People are switched on to their Facebook and smartphones but off from their family and dreams. Rather than being connected, I think we're becoming more and more disconnected – from ourselves. The problem isn't really technology. It's emptiness and lack of focus.

It's easy to blunt our awareness of life with background noise, food, social media or whatever else. Our point is, albeit a harsh-sounding one, what if busyness is the easy option? As Robert Holden suggests, if there's something missing in your life, it's probably you.[2]

> Interesting analogy?
>
> *Like sharks, we must keep moving to stay alive and, as with sharks, the grin is false.*

If I ask you, 'What do you think is the only thing that can fill that gaping "you-shaped" hole?' the answer is intuitively obvious yet we continue to plough on filling it with 'stuff', busyness and social media. I used to have what Guy Browning calls 'Irritable Bastard Syndrome',[3] brought on by being jolted from my sleep with my to-do list breathing down my neck. You probably know the feeling, it was like starting my day off with a panic attack. There were the things I felt I should do: write a book, go on a diet, do some sit-ups, learn to play the piano, read for pleasure, set some mole traps in my garden ... and things I absolutely had to do: go to work, empty the bins, watch my son play rugby, get my daughter to footy training, reply to the most urgent emails ...

Somewhere between 'should' and 'must', there was this low-grade grumble pushing me along. The grumbling I saw as a necessary evil to fire-up my willpower. Low-level negativity was my fuel. No wonder I was spluttering! But no matter how much I'd get done, it never quite seemed like enough. I didn't have time to be happy! My to-do list would sometimes scream so loudly that it'd keep me awake at night. I kept a notepad and pen by my bed to write stuff down.

I'd wake up at some ungodly hour, scribble something in the dark and then drop back to sleep. After a fitful night I'd wake to a to-do list that had lengthened during the night – I couldn't remember doing it but there it was – a nightmarish reminder in my own scrawly handwriting of how much I'd failed to do yesterday and how much I had to do today. The alarm wasn't so much of a wake-up call, more an emergency siren heralding another day of manic full-on action. I'd stumble out of bed, open the curtains and there were a dozen fresh mole hills, both real and metaphorical.

As is often the case, it's the little things that add up to being a big thing we call 'life'. The problem with my old life was that being propelled by low-level grumbling wasn't just affecting my own quality of life, it was impacting on people much more important than myself.

Let me explain. The old 'standard' version of me was perfectly fine, if a little stressed, mildly irritable and counting down to the weekend. I'd be hunched at my laptop, clearing the day's emails, most often until way past bedtime. I'd been delivering training all day so this was the only time I had to catch up with customers. At around 9pm my son would wander into the back-bedroom of an office, with his pyjamas on and a teddy tucked under his arm and yawn, 'Dad, it's 9 o'clock. Can you read me a story?'

I'd be half way through an urgent email to a hugely important client. Without breaking away from my laptop I'd mutter, 'I'm busy mate. Can it wait?'

'Not really dad. It's 9 o'clock, dad. Bedtime. I've done my teeth and had a wee. I need a story.'

Irritated, I'd break away from my half-finished email and swivel on my chair, facing my lad. 'For heaven's sake,' I'd sigh, 'You're 23! At what point are you going to start reading your own bedtime stories?'

Sorry, that last sentence is a cheap gag. He's four. Let's try that bit again ...

Irritated, I'd break away from my half-finished email and swivel on my chair, facing my lad. 'For heaven's sake,' I'd sigh. 'I'm reaaaally busy. If I must! But I've only got time for a short chapter, okay?' And I'd stomp off to Ollie's bedroom where he'd wriggle into bed and I'd sit there, find the book from last night where the page was turned over, and I'd read a chapter. My aim was to get it done quickly and efficiently, so I could get back to the emails. The result was that I'd read it fast – in fact you could test me on what I'd just read and I wouldn't have a clue because I wasn't really listening, I was just getting it done, as quickly as possible. And if Ollie wasn't concentrating I'd sometimes turn two pages over at once, trying to skip a boring section. I'd get to the end of the chapter, snap the book shut and stumble back downstairs to the half-finished email. Thank goodness that's out of the way. It'd been a chore – a thing on my to-do list – a pain in the backside.

Cut to the new version of me. Before you read it, please note that just as *Jaws* isn't really about a shark, this isn't about bedtime stories. It's about the small changes that make a huge difference to your life. I'm still busy. I've still got too many things on my to-do list and not enough time to clear them. I'm still doing emails at 9pm and, yes, I know it's easy to argue that I shouldn't be, but the truth is that I am. And my son still comes in at 9pm with, 'Dad, it's bedtime. Can you do me a story?'

The new version of me is, quite frankly, delighted to be asked. Irrespective of whatever email I'm engrossed in, there is nothing more important than this moment and this relationship. 'Sure thing li'l dude,' I smile. We skip upstairs. Ollie wriggles in, duvet up to his chin, eyes shining in excitement and I pick the book off the bedside table. Before I start reading – and this is crucial – I ask myself how would the best dad in the world read this story? The answer is so very simple; like he really wanted to. Like it was the most important story in the world. And that's how it gets read. The baddie has a baddie voice, the goody has a goody voice, the action leaps off the page, the funny bits are proper belly laughs and I don't want to skip a single sentence. I leave it on a cliff-hanger – *dun dun duuuuun* – I can't wait to find out what happens next ...

We have a cuddle and I retreat back to the half-finished email, no longer with a sense of *phew, thank goodness that's out of the way* but much more with a sense of *wow, that was amazing.* Reading the bedtime story has become the highlight of my day, a joy and privilege, instead of the low-light. The only tiny change I've made is that I've removed it from my 'to-do' list and placed it firmly on my 'to-be' list. Small change, big impact. It's these tiny changes that add up to a rejuvenation of your relationships and have a domino effect on your life.

I'd dare to suggest that your to-do list occupies most of your attention. You'll be rushing headlong through a long list of things that need ticking off and, while these things are important, they are miniscule in relation to your 'to-be' list. I'd argue that your to-be list is a million times more important because it brings you to the perpetual question – *who am I being while I'm doing this task?*

In the case of the bedtime story, am I being irritated, negative and hassled, or am I being upbeat, patient and loving? It's simple really. I filled the donut-shaped emptiness in my life with loads of 'me at my best'.

In the modern-day vernacular, I think they call it a no-brainer?

Are You Wearing Your 'Eating Trousers'?

And on to our final apocalyptic rider, 'enoughness'. It's interesting that if you ask *Who wants to be a millionaire?* to an assembly hall of children, 100 per cent will enthusiastically raise their hands, whereas about half will raise their hands to *Who wants to be happy?*

So let's change the question to something much more interesting: *What would you rather have, '£1 million' or 'not be dead'?*

It might take a nano-second but most people will instinctively go for option 2. In fact, I can probably raise the stakes and offer you £10 million and you'd still opt for the alive option?

Is this some stupid play on words, a silly mind game, or simply a reminder of the value you place on life? It seems that most people forget how awesome merely being alive is so consider this chapter as a massive reminder, a huge yellow ribbon tied around the tallest of life's oak trees. You're here, reading these words. Therefore you're alive, you're educated and that's a decent starting point because we've already deduced that it's worth a million quid to you. But chances are that sometimes you don't feel very alive? The weather and work pressures and, despite playing my silly million-pound game, your real bank balance is in the red.

Have you noticed that all the really big breakthroughs (fire, the wheel, the pyramids, the printing press, Velcro, pop-tarts, Tupperware) all happened before social media had been invented? And there's no way 'child-genius' Mozart would have found time to compose all those classic advertisement tunes if he'd had an Xbox. As for the famous Thomas Edison story in which it apparently took him eight years and 1000 failures before he eventually invented the lightbulb. Really? I'm afraid the modern workplace would have got rid of him after, say, ten failures. He would have been called in to the manager's office – *Look here Tommy, you're a nice lad and all, but you're just not the right fit for us. We need instant winners, see.*

My work takes me out and about so I'm often in hotels which leaves me battling the temptation of the 'all-you-can-eat' breakfast. Note, it's not 'eat-what-you-need' brekky, it's an *all-you-CAN-eat-get-your-money's-worth-schmuck* culinary gauntlet. Your brain tricks you because, many hundreds of generations ago, food was in short supply. If you had some, you'd scoff it, very quickly. We gorged ourselves to bulk up for the thin days ahead. And you don't have to go back very far – for example, First World War soldiers averaged 5 foot 5 inches, because they were malnourished as children.

Our ancestors indulged in impossible dreams of exactly the same conditions that we find ourselves in today ... warmth, safety, food, drink, comfort ... but Mother Nature has designed us to operate as perpetual dissatisfaction machines. In an ironic twist of evolution, for the first time ever we are living amid abundance but our minds are still pre-programmed to fear scarcity. We are built to seek comfort, shelter and food but are not designed to have them all the time.

We are drowning in choice. Which brings us onto a plethora of happiness findings that come under the generic heading of 'personal responsibility'. Abundance is laid out before you like the aforementioned all-you-can-eat breakfast buffet. You have more choices to make than anyone else in the history of human beings.

That's liberating but also highly pressurized because, unbeknown to you, your life has become the sum of your choices. There really isn't anyone else you can blame. Sure, it would be nice to cast the blame on fate, or your job, genes or circumstances. Maybe even the government or God? You can point the finger at them all but it'll do you no good. I figure that if nobody's coming to rescue me, I will have to rescue myself. That means I had to start making good choices, not just about buffet breakfasts but about attitudes, emotions, behaviours and thoughts. Yes, all those messy innards I alluded to earlier.

It's easy to join the zombie army, sleepwalking through a world of busyness and distraction. It's even easier to overdose on life's buffet. Being happy is about learning some new mental strategies, but it's equally about knowing when enough is enough. Our primitive brain keeps digging us deeper into the moreish arms race. Waiting for everybody else to change is pointless. You'll die waiting. We dare you to be happy with what you've already got.

Top Tips

1. Wake up! *Hellooooo!* You spend a seventh of your life on Mondays so snap out of the zombie-like trance of *Mondays are bad and Fridays are ace.* They're equal. It's all in your head. Next Monday, go into work with your Friday attitude and see what happens.

2. Stop skimming the surface of life. Do less, but better.
3. Ask 'how would the best version of me tackle this situation?' and then act accordingly.
4. Be the best bedtime story reader, ever!
5. Stop starting. If, like me, you can't just have one biscuit or one chocolate (*they're open so they need eating*) then stop opening them, aka 'stop starting'.
6. Quit the blame game and rid yourself of 'irritable bastard syndrome' by taking charge of your attitude. Positivity for 11 consecutive days please. Oh, and report back.

♡ marshmallows &
unicorns

Chapter 3

MEADOWS OF MARSHMALLOWS AND UNICORNS

●●●●●●

In which we wake up and smell the coffee. Mmmmm, breathe it in, the aroma of the freshly brewed Colombian Arabica, kick-starting your day in the exotic world of marshmallows and unicorns.

We start by exploring the 'Golden Circle' (like Thailand's 'Golden Triangle' but without the weed) before moving on to that old psychological ding-dong of *will-power* versus *won't-power* and *hedonism* versus *eudemonism*.

Then we explore the 50 shades of happiness, from the mild snogging of *hygge* to full-blown whips and gimp masks of 'woohoo' – and all things in-between.

We then shower off before explaining why kids hate walking in wonderful cities. As always we tail it with a big thought and a series of top tips, one of which might cause the neighbours' curtains to twitch.

Before the off, this is a beautiful land with lots of opportunities for photos. But, if you're stepping outside of the vehicle please be careful. See that rainbow-coloured turd? The unicorns are friendly, but they shit everywhere.

••••••

ONWARDS ...

••••••

••••••

GÖKOTTA (SWEDISH): WAKING UP EARLY TO HEAR THE FIRST BIRDS SING.

••••••

Itchy Guy

We depart the depths of Zombie Land to reach the warm uplands of a happier place, where unicorns frolic, rainbows paint the sky and it's marshmallows for breakfast, lunch and high tea. A land where everyone skips into work, a joyous strengths-based culture where staff willingly go the extra mile in a quest to make their customers and colleagues go 'wow!' A world of purpose-driven, gleaming teeth, white-eyed energy.

Check your zombie face in at hotel reception because you won't be needing it here. Yes indeed dear traveller, welcome to the world as we think it should be.

Before we unpick the ridiculousness of the previous paragraphs, let's introduce you to a fact and another new word. On the Japanese island of Okinawa there is, apparently, no word for 'retirement'. But they have a lovely word *Ikagai* (pronounced 'itchy-guy') which is defined as the reason you get up in the morning. Being in tune with your purpose provides motivational fuel, and if you're wanting to become a grand-master of the concept, you might want to consider helping others tune into theirs.

Happiness: Instant or Percolated?

Setting happiness as your aim dooms you to failure because, once again, you're falling into the trap of setting it as an end goal. Happiness is more a by-product of you engaging in moments, relationships, strengths and hobbies and if you aim to make others happy you will experience the side-effect of you catching it too.

The upshot is that it's nigh on impossible to command yourself to be happy. There will be times when you need to exert pressure on yourself to 'wear a smile' and 'tackle a challenge head on'. This will involve giving yourself a bit of a talking to (out loud or in your head, it's the same thing) and this pep-talk will sustain your positivity, short-term. But willpower works like a muscle and becomes fatigued.

If you're relying on willpower to make you happy, you're doomed to fail. Willpower will fuel your positivity, but it's always a battle. Try using willpower to resist cakes? I can do it (sometimes) but it takes effort and makes me sad. That's because if I need willpower, I'm battling my internal dialogue. I haven't really decided to change.

We're not sure what the opposite of willpower is, so we're going to call it 'won't power'. Here's an eerie example. I was recently visiting my mum in hospital and, as I walked in, there was the usual gaggle of pyjama-clad patients, some in wheelchairs, some wheeling drips around with them, congregated at the hospital door, desperately sucking on cigarettes.

It was a properly freezing cold day. One of them was a pale skinny bloke, sitting in a wheelchair with a blanket over his knees, shivering to his bone marrow. His lips were blue, presumably from the cold but I guess he could have been admitted for 'blue lip disease'? Look folks, I'm not a medic.

Anyhow, he had smoked his cigarette down to its final centimetre, doing that expert smoker thing where you finish it off by doing the three-finger hold, eking out the last bit of nicotine before he went back to the ward. That paragraph sounds judgemental. It's not. It's factual. As I walked past, the shivering chap grabbed my arm. 'Scuse me mate,' he wheezed, 'Can you wheel me back to my ward? It's freezing and the nurse won't be here to collect me for another 20 minutes.'

Not a problem. I wheeled him inside and we had a bit of banter. I pressed the lift button and we waited. 'Brass monkeys out there today,' I said. 'Almost cold enough for you to consider giving up smoking.'

'I have mate,' he said. 'I gave up two days ago.'

We ascended to the fourth floor in stunned silence. He and the nurse thanked me as I dropped him off in ward 404, the cancer ward.

He was a nice chap but I'm still wondering about that conversation? It was real. The guy who 30 seconds before had been dragging on a cigarette was swearing blind that he'd given up. He's a classic example of his instant happiness outweighing his long-term joy.

We'll use big words in a minute but, for now, let's liken happiness to a cup of coffee. You can have an instant coffee right now. Flick the kettle on, a spoonful of granules and bingo – it's instant but a bit crap. Or you can wait a bit longer and have proper coffee. You have to trade off a bit of time but if you can wait five minutes you get a decent zinging mugful that makes your pupils dilate.

Ask my blue-lipped smoker friend how his enjoyment of smoking has affected his life's happiness. Ask a 35-stone woman how her love of Ben & Jerry's has affected her long-term happiness. Ask a crack addict how his love of an instant high is affecting his lifetime joy. We all love a bit of pleasure and we're not saying cut out the happiness shortcuts, merely that quite a few lead to literal dead ends.

50 Shades of Happiness

Thought for the day

Happiness is a feeling to tap into, not an outcome of events.

If you're a reader of a certain age you will also have noticed that happiness morphs through the phases of your life. When you were six, happiness came from unicorns, rainbows, trampolining and cheese strings. Then, as a teenager, it shape-shifted into parties, staying up late and playing spin the bottle. Most of those will have fallen by the wayside by middle age – trampolining makes your bones rattle, cheese strings make you vomit, but you do still quite like a rainbow and wouldn't mind a game of spin the bottle – and happiness has shifted to 'reading a book' or 'Sunday lunch with the family'. As bizarre as it sounds, if I could go back and whisper to the 18-year-old me that, 'Guess what, when you're 50, you'll actually prefer to stay in on a Saturday night', the teenage me would have laughed uproariously. It was unthinkable. I'd have been devastated to imagine my life could turn out to be so ... boring?

There's a Danish word, *hygge* (pronounced 'hoo-ga') for which there is no direct English translation. The best approximation might be 'comfort'. Coming in on a winter's morning to a steaming mug of hot chocolate – for me, that is. Your *hygge* will be different.

Happiness comes in all sorts of varieties – from the quiet contentment of *hygge*, to the more noticeable Cheshire Cat grin, to full blown 'dancing around the house naked' – and from an assortment of sources. If we dare to explore the upper end of the spectrum, way beyond 'Cheshire Cat' into 'woohoo' territory, you will find 'joy'. This is a real biggy. First up, it's not easy to experience joy on your own. If you think of your top ten most joyous moments, they will almost certainly have been shared experiences (and, at a guess, most probably without Wi-Fi?) Joy is a difficult state to describe – somewhere beyond the ordinary swell of happiness into a feeling of unbridled pleasure that is often momentary. Joy is special because of its rarity. Anthony Seldon elucidates on the quantum leap from happiness to joy, describing joy as being immersed in love to a point where nothing can impregnate the moment and, somewhat prosaically, as a sense of coming home after a holiday, to the place and people you love the most.[4]

The secret of enlightenment is to be able to access that feeling as often as possible. Theoretically, the feeling is possible even in the midst of sorrow or stress. As Anthony Seldon suggests, joy can be all of the aforementioned (cheese strings or Sunday lunch but, heaven forbid, not together) but tends to be less about 'me me me' and more about being spiritually connected.

Please don't fall into the trap of confusing spirituality with religion. Spirituality, for us three at least, means feeling connected. To experience joy, others' happiness is more important than our own and our aim becomes to serve. Joy is often experienced in those moments of observing other people being happy. My father-in-law is a good example. At family get-togethers he often takes a back seat, sitting and observing while his daughters and their families get on like a house on fire. He often reaches for his hankie and wipes away a tear. His joy lies in observing us having fun.

But of course, you already know all of the above. We all choose our lives. As we learned in Zombie Land, what and who we are today is a result of past choices. Admittedly, they might not have felt like choices at the time but they were. We may choose to blame other people or circumstances or indeed, ourselves. So a great place to start is to take responsibility for where we are and resolve to work on the only thing we can really change, which is, of course, ourselves.

And that, dear reader, is where it can all come crashing down!

Top Tips

1. Find your purpose, and help others connect with theirs. If you're struggling, get a piece of A4 paper, turn it landscape, and write a single sentence that sums up what you're all about. What, at your core, do you stand for? What kind of person are you when you're being your best self? That sentence is likely to be your purpose.
2. Willpower and happiness don't mix. Stop trying to be happy and start allowing yourself to be so.
3. Experience more happiness, the Danish way. Work out what your hoo-ga is, and do more of it.
4. Appreciate that happiness changes as you change. This is why your kids don't ever want to come on a countryside walk or traipse around Venice. (*It's just canals. So boooring.*)
5. Grow your happiness roots. That means sourcing it eudemonically, via goals, purpose and relationships. Hedonism is fine, sometimes, but don't let it kill you.
6. Oh, and keep on scratchin' that itchy guy itch.

Chapter 4
MONEY MOUNTAIN

• • • • • •

In which we start with flying lizards and end with a philosophical headache.

Here we take the money/happiness relationship through some counselling and have a look at a happiness survey that actually makes you happy (unless you're a banker).

Then we're off to the uplands of Money Mountain, via Bhutan and Ikea, glancing at the newspaper columns along the way. We look at how we keep score of national success and at how George Best kept score of his own happiness.

Skipping the Central African Republic, and skirting Syria, we check out the so-called 'Easterlin Effect' with the message of stop comparing and start shining. To finish, we look at what happiness is actually worth to you (roughly an arm and a leg) and why sex is so confusing (should it involve cake and is it socks on or off?).

Anyhow, strap yourself in for a tour of Money Mountain. You might spot a couple of naughty words and there's something else you'll notice in this land – lots of green grass. See it? Right over there in the distance? Bizarrely, it's never under your feet.

Warning: the terrain is steep in places and there are vertical drops on either side.

Hold tight. We're off up Money Mountain …

••••••

IKTSUARPOK (INUIT): DESCRIBES THE WORRY THAT NOBODY WILL COME TO YOUR PARTY, ROUGHLY AKIN TO 'ANXIOUSLY WAITING FOR FRIENDS TO COME TO YOUR HOUSE AND REPEATEDLY GOING OUTSIDE TO SEE IF THEY HAVE ARRIVED YET'.

••••••

Altitude Sickness

Money and happiness – it's a confusing relationship. I think one-hit-wonders, The Flying Lizards, got the modern world just about spot on when they acknowledged that although the best things in life are free, you can give them to the birds and bees because what they really want is money (there was a lot of *ooooooooooing* too).

So, basically, stick your freebies and give me hard cash because hard cash enables me to buy stuff. Rock & roller David Lee-Roth wasn't a million miles away when he suggested money can't buy you happiness, but it can buy you a yacht big enough to pull up right alongside it.

Chasing the cash gives rise to what Jamie Smart calls the 'experience economy' characterized by people who are so time-poor that the quality of the experience becomes important.[5] So Starbucks' simple offering of allowing you to scroll through your emails while sipping a Java chip yak's milk Frappuccino and tucking into a lemon and poppy seed muffin, in an oasis of calm, becomes £15 well spent.

The internet is awash with happiness surveys. For instance, the so-called 'Career Happiness Index'[6] produces a league table of happy occupations. Florists and gardeners are top (87 per cent of them are happy), with hairdressers and plumbers close behind. May I point out the bleeding obvious – none are particularly high earning jobs. Just to prove that the universe works in wondrous ways, bankers came bottom with only 44 per cent of them experiencing happiness. This survey actually made me happy!

If you enjoy your job, you're luckier than most. I've met a lot of people who work overtime at a job they hate to get promoted so they can work twice as hard doing something they hate even more. The next pay rise temporarily papers over the cracks of discontentment.

Or you can go self-employed and boldly strike out on your own. I did that ten years ago and my mates were green with envy. 'You can have holidays whenever you want!' swooned one. 'And "working from home" isn't exactly "work" is it?' said another. 'It'll be the life of Riley.' Now I'm not sure who Riley was but judging from my experience, Riley must have been someone who worked 14 hours a day, six days a week before slackening off to ten hours on Sundays.

And just to close the loop, I Googled 'Larry' as in the 'happy as Larry' saying. Who the heck was he? Turns out that Larry Foley was an Australian boxer who was punching people in Victorian times. Larry never lost a fight and won a whopping £1000 for his last bout. So, you see, the myth is busted right there – stick that in your philosophical pipe and smoke it – money made Larry happy.

Apart from the slightly bonkers Himalayan Kingdom of Bhutan that measures its success as gross domestic happiness (a crazy idea, most likely brought on by altitude sickness), elsewhere, economists rule the airwaves. There's always a finance section on the news. We're told that a rise in GDP is good because GDP is a posh way of saying 'national income', the sum total of everything we're all earning, lumped together. By this calculation, divorce is good. All that lovely money the lawyers will make and the extra house that'll be needed when one of the divorcees is forced out. No wonder IKEA's booming! Ooh, and don't forget counselling for the kids. Similarly, car crashes are brilliant news for the economy; all those repairs and a loan car and whiplash claim. Or better still, write it off and buy a new one, with finance. Yum yum. And the economy loves depressed people. All that comfort food, those busy doctors' surgeries and soaring pharma sales. Or why not book into rehab? *Kerching!*

It's not money making the world go round, it's misery!

There's a standard formula that determines the size of a newspaper's finance section. It is in direct proportion to readership income levels multiplied by their perceived financial intelligence. So the red tops have next to nothing, unless they can wangle a picture of a sexy lady underneath the headline 'Marks & Spencer blame bad weather on poor sales of swimwear' kind of thing. So the rule of thumb is that the finance section of the tabloids doesn't carry the biggest news, just the most picture friendly. Their financial page consists of emails such as 'Dear newspaper, I've won £50 on the bingo and don't want my husband to find out or he'll drink it. What should I do?'

Broadsheets swing the other way, often crediting their readership with bags more financial nous than they actually have. They have whole financial sections (a paper within a paper) that seem predicated on the belief that if you read a newspaper that makes your arms ache, it should also make your head ache, so they list a bewildering array of shares, bonds, ISAs, Gilts, FTSE 100, Dow, Dax, Hang Seng, $/£, euro/£, premium bonds, coffee, beef, cereals, wine, art, Chicago hog prices and gold. Their letters page is 'Dear Sir, I have a £3 million nest-egg and want to invest in something off-shore. I'm looking for low initial charges and a draw-down option with medium-term capital accumulation. Not overly keen on Panama. Any advice?'

George and the Pauper

Data collector Neli Esipova[7] has travelled the world asking folk about happiness. In a Sri Lankan slum her 'data source' was a thin, middle-aged woman in rags, squatting beside a charcoal-burning stove. Neli asked the woman her standard question of, 'On a scale of one to ten, how satisfied are you with your life?'

'Ten,' smiled the woman, explaining that she had a son who respected her, a husband who loved her, enough money to buy food, some dye for her hair and a little left over for the church.

So much for GDP which says *if it's got a price-tag, we'll measure it*. Have you ever tried to measure happiness, love, community or self-esteem?

We're taught that money makes the world go round but also that it can't buy love. This brings me to the classic George Best scene – for the younger generation, Bestie, a bit of a looker, played for Man Utd back in the day. The footballing lothario is sitting in his hotel suite, bottle of Moet on ice, wads of tenners on the bedside table, about to seduce Miss World. Someone bursts in, takes a look at what's going on, shakes his head and says, 'George, where did it all go wrong?'

George was your classic 'live life to the full' kind of guy, with scant regard for longevity. His strategy was to cram oodles of instant gratification into his life to the point where he actually got a new liver just so he could keep on drinking. While I'm not advocating you do that, it's hard not to have a sneaking admiration for his single-minded approach to instant, no-holds-barred happiness. George lived at the peak of Money Mountain and, along the way, had become addicted to hedonism. He wanted happiness, by any means, and he wanted it now. I speak of George in the past tense. His pursuit of instant and extreme gratification took its toll. If he'd lived a less intense life he might still be with us. But what a massive gamble. Sod's Law dictates that if George had restrained himself – less Moet, fewer Miss Worlds – he'd have gone under a bus at age 46?

As we learned in the previous chapter, the longer and more winding happiness route is via the over-complicatedly worded *eudemonism*. This is a more measured approach to happiness that restricts our access to George's excesses. Most of us make do with less Moet and fewer Miss Worlds (I'll skip the vexed question of what would we do in that hotel room if we were in George's position?) We restrict our spending, squirrelling a few coins away for retirement. It worries us who's going to wipe our bottoms and give us a wash-down when we're 98.

George wasn't burdened with such worries. Instead, he was burdened with money, good looks and, most of all, opportunity.

After pondering for some time, I've come to the conclusion that money might not buy happiness but it can certainly buy you comfort, ease, choice and possibility. It remains the number one best thing I know for putting food on the table and being able to turn up the central heating.

As for not being able to buy love? Perhaps. But it can buy a couple of long-haul flights to somewhere with palm trees.

On balance, you don't need to be an expert to work out that money isn't a guarantee but it enhances your probability of happiness.

Go Compare

Science reveals a link between money and happiness, but the link weakens as income grows. In essence, people on very low incomes will experience increases in happiness, but only up to a certain point. The exact point is debateable, but roughly equates to a household income of £50k.[8]

A more salient point is that it tends not to be your absolute income that matters, but how you compare with those around you. So in the highly paid world of premiership football, when your club signs a new player on £250k a week, you start grumbling at your measly £220k. *How unfair. I hate this club. They treat me like a dog.* Yes, it's crazy, but that's how we operate.

This introduces a big quandary as far as governments are concerned because happiness becomes subject to the so-called Easterlin Effect. This is how it works – in international happiness league tables it is true that, generally speaking, citizens of rich countries rate as happier than those from poor ones. Not only are they rich, but most of the top ten countries are also a bit chilly, the current top five being Norway, Denmark, Iceland, Switzerland and Finland (UK is 19th but a smidgeon warmer).[9]

The bottom five are a whole lot poorer but red hot. From bottom up they read Central African Republic, Burundi, Tanzania, Syria and Rwanda.

So, other than *don't book your summer holidays in Central African Republic*, what does this tell us? Probably not as much as you might imagine. I don't want to belittle whatever's going on in sub-Saharan Africa, but the Easterlin Effect suggests that it's very difficult to raise what we'll call 'gross domestic happiness' because, as the economy grows and everyone earns more money, our relative pecking order remains the same so we don't feel any happier.

Comparison is a double-edged happiness phenomenon. It can be motivating, but it can also make you miserable. Instead of arguing that you need to 'stop comparing yourself with others' (that's hard to do because your brain is wired to do it) we'll make the point that competitive and cooperative feelings can and do co-exist within the same person, and neither feeling is necessarily superior. It's learning when to *use* each feeling that counts. Adam Galinksy and Maurice Schweitzer write that 'when it comes to using social comparison to boost your own motivation, here is the key rule to keep in mind: Seek favourable comparisons if you want to feel happier, and seek unfavourable comparisons if you want to push yourself harder'.[10] To paraphrase, you may not be able to quit your social-comparison habit, but you can learn to make it work for you.

Part of the double-edgedness is that our in-built sense of social comparison effectively gives us a sense that the grass is always greener over there. And for 'green grass' you can substitute material comparisons of car, lifestyle, income, holidays and such like. Or your neighbour can have better behaved kids than your own unruly bunch. Or a sexier husband. Or a wife with bigger boobs. Or they go on holiday to America and you make do with Whitby.

The rabbit out of the happiness hat is to keep your own grass lush and verdant. Incidentally, have you noticed that all-too-often your social comparison works upwards? If you are struggling to let go of the 'grass is always greener' illusion, why not try working it down the social spectrum. I mean, not only is Whitby the most fab seaside town in England and with the best fish and chips on the entire planet, but it's also better than a Travelodge in Grimsby. And a Travelodge in Grimsby is definitely better than sleeping on a park bench in Goole. And your children, as unruly as they might sometimes be, are actually a massive bonus in your life and, without putting too fine a point on it, some people are unable to have children at all. Your grass is not just green, it's fluorescent emerald.

> Interesting thought about 'the good old days'
>
> *Every good speech has its day and Harold Macmillan's 'you've never had it so good' fits modern-day Britain to a tee.*

While we're on Money Mountain, where numbers are everything, it's worth glancing at The University of London's Institute of Education report that has attempted to put a monetary value on intangibles. Get this ...

- Seeing friends and relatives is equivalent to a pay rise of £64k a year
- Chatting to nice neighbours is worth £37k a year
- Getting married is worth £70k a year
- And the biggy: excellent health is estimated to be worth £300k a year to you.[11]

I sincerely hope you can tick some of the boxes above? Of course, it's easy to pick holes or make cheap jibes (the researcher has clearly never met my wife, etc.), but the wider point about relationships and health is staggering. So here's a very big point. We are ingratitude spotters, fixating on all the stuff that we haven't yet got. We spend oodles of hard-earned cash chasing trinkets.

Taking the argument to the extreme, I guess you could trade in your family, friends, neighbours and good health and collect £451k? And you'd be nearly half a million pounds richer, but so much poorer.

Here's something else to factor into the happiness equation – in the Western world, I'm not sure we actually understand the true meaning of 'poverty'? My kids' school sponsors an orphanage in Uganda and every year a delegation of sixth formers go out there to paint, repair, clean and teach. Of course, it's not about acquiring basic DIY skills, it's 100 per cent about experiencing proper poverty and getting the kids to feel supremely grateful for all the things that are handed to them on a plate. They return to Blighty with a renewed zest for their own home, a comfy bed, a superb school, a mum, three meals a day, their Xbox, books, Wi-Fi, a temperate climate, shoes, duvets, flushing toilets, chips, computers, running water, tarmac, soft loo roll, supermarkets, the NHS, hair straighteners (that tends to be the girls, but not always) ... anyway, you get my point.

> **Win : Win?**
>
> *Sod the expense, and this is a serious suggestion – send every teenager to the Central African Republic for a week. CAR needs the foreign currency and our kids need perspective.*

Back to The Flying Lizards line, 'the best things in life are free' – it's easy to argue that this is platitudinal twaddle peddled by those with enough money to purchase an education that included some decent philosophy classes.

Being deadly serious for a moment, why not take five minutes off, grab a pen and paper and list the top ten happiest moments of your life. In fact, we'll create some space for you below. Go on, do it, right now.

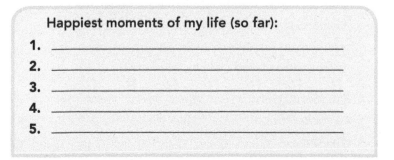

Happiest moments of my life (so far):

1. _____
2. _____
3. _____
4. _____
5. _____

6. _____
7. _____
8. _____
9. _____
10. _____

I'd hazard that there are no products on your list? It will consist entirely of experiences – *with other people.*

A short story about love

A loving mother was walking down a promenade holding hands with her gorgeous four-year-old son when suddenly a rogue wave crashed over the barrier and washed the little lad out to sea.

Can you image how she must have felt at that moment? Her only son, taken so cruelly?

Then suddenly another wave crashed over the promenade and as it retreated back – there he was, soaked but safe. The lad gently reached out a trembling hand and held his mummy tight.

She looked down at her sea-soaked son's smiling face and thought, 'F****** hell where's his b****** hat gone.'

Digging Deep

So, the big hairy question that needs addressing is: what if we are built to seek lasting happiness but not to find it? What if that's all part of the plan?

We are a tangle of emotions, some positive and some negative, but all pushing us onwards, to live, love, reproduce and die having inched our species forwards towards happiness and away from unhappiness. Deep down we have a belief that we can't be happy yet – there are a few more boxes to tick.

If we begin to piece some of the learning together, it would seem that to be truly happy we have to switch off our factory setting of 'social comparison'. To throw a bit of Freud at you, your 'id' needs taming. For those of you not versed in Freud, the id is that hedonistic part of you that wants to do things and do them NOW! It doesn't want to wait. Oh, and it's rather primal. It doesn't care who's watching or who you upset. It wants sex. And cakes. Preferably at the same time.

Its fervour is normally cooled by the ego. This is the boring part of your personality that is shy and retiring. It tells you not to eat cake and not to have sex (and, if you do, to do it in the dark and keep your socks on).

As we discovered in the all-you-can-eat buffet of Zombie Land, this is the golden age of the id. It's rampant and untamed. If you'll allow me to bastardize Churchill, never have so many wanted so much so badly. And never have we wanted to be satisfied as quickly.

55

Nowadays advertising is viral. Like a disease! Its aim is to create dissatisfaction with your current lifestyle so you feel the urge to upgrade to a better sofa, newer car, sexier laptop or a better pair of breasts. Life is a progression, not from young-to-old but from desire-to-desire. Perhaps Seneca was right when he said, 'It is not the man who has too little but the man who craves more that is poor.' Or that sage of all things mammon, the philosopher/F1 driver Jenson Button: 'It doesn't matter how much money you've got, or how many connections, there's always something you want that's out of reach.'

If the evidence is correct and people who desire more money or material wealth tend to be unhappier, a celebrity-obsessed world of retail therapy is setting itself up to fail. And yet we remain totally convinced. There's a voice inside of you right now, screaming at me. Are you trying to tell me that buying stuff won't make me happy because it bloody well will!

I have a theory that 500 years down the line they'll be looking back at this time in history and chuckling at how we let money and jobs define our lives and how we heaped praise on public figures but forgot to praise the real heroes in our lives.

What does our climb to the top of Money Mountain ultimately teach us? Hopefully, it will educate that inner shouty voice to be less shrill. Maybe it teaches us to be happy with what we've got, rather than falling for the marketing con of lusting after whatever they're pushing?

Or maybe it's much bigger than that? Suppose what we're searching for amongst the branches can only be found amongst the roots? Crikey, that's a biggy. We'll drop it in there and come back to it later.

Top Tips

1. 'Stuff' will bring you instant but short-lived happiness. It can also bring debt. To squeeze more value from your happiness pound, spend it on experiences.
2. Better still, save your cash and invest in relationships (aka, 'spend more time with the people you love').
3. The average hug lasts 2.1 seconds. In order for the love to transfer, a hug needs to last 7 seconds or longer (but don't count out loud as it spoils the effect).
4. Be a florist or a gardener. Grow something.
5. Stop comparing yourself with airbrushed perfection (if you absolutely have to compare, try comparing downwards).
6. Appreciate what you have rather than lusting after what you haven't.

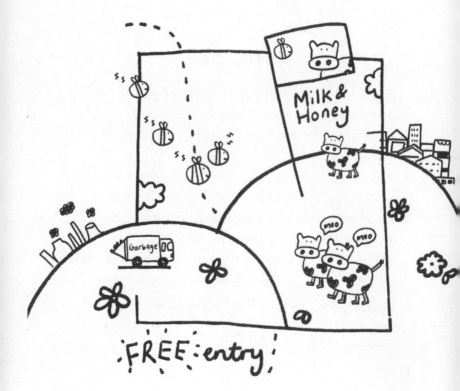

Chapter 5

THE LAND OF MILK AND HONEY

• • • • • •

In which we avoid the crowds by venturing from the well-trodden path.

In olden times, mystical elders lived here but they died out, and in the modern world everyone's so busy climbing to the top of Money Mountain, that they don't take time to look at the view.

This is the land where East meets West and where Mondays are valued the same as Fridays. We look at why 10-gallon hats might need to be extended to 20 gallons and, continuing the Texan theme, we learn a happiness lesson as we descend into Dallas Airport.

We look at 'infomaniacs' and 'musterbators' as well as introducing the Dalai Lama's nemesis, the voluptuous 'Dolly Lama'. But all in all, this land is a rather earnest place. If you 'get it', it will change your life and, what's more, entry to 'right now' is free.

You will have heard the word 'lepidopterist' but you're not quite sure are you? Are they stamp collectors, maybe? All will be revealed in a back-to-basics humdinger of a chapter that also includes garbage trucks and gratitude.

See that flag? Yes, the one with a cow and a bee. Ladies and gentlemen, check out the lush green grass, it's always under your feet. Welcome to the curious Land of Milk and Honey, a chapter that's cleverer than it seems, the land of mindfulness like you've never heard it described before…

••••••

GULA (SPANISH): THE DESIRE TO EAT SIMPLY FOR THE TASTE.

••••••

Nobody Ever Thinks They're Stupid – It's Part of the Stupidity

First up, we are not anti-capitalist. We are not advocating a back-to-basics agrarian society in which we shun possessions and all sit, cross-legged, chanting our gratitude for the roasted mealworms we're about to eat. We drive nice cars, live in nice houses and have wallowed in as much materialism as the next person.

However, as our coach tour left Money Mountain, you'll have noticed it was a solid drive through vast industrial estates where factories are churning out stuff. You see, these social climbers need possessions. In fact, an insatiable desire to have more stuff than the Joneses is what fuels them in their climb. Did you notice all the swanky new nailbars? We think this might be because there's a lot of clinging to the sides of Money Mountain by your fingertips?

And if you looked to your left there were vast warehouses, once again, further than the eye can see. When the residents have tired of their stuff they need somewhere to put it, so they rent huge warehouses to store the material possessions that have failed to make them happy. This fuels the factories and retail outlets because they can then sell more stuff to fill the space that's been created. It's a near perfect system (just so long as nobody stops and thinks about it too much).

And there are some of the offices. This is where the marketing teams reside. Their job is to make you want the stuff and we've got the best marketing people in the world. Ever wondered why you've got 57 pairs of shoes? And as we crossed the border did you see that family trudging back from the retail park, laden with bags, with haggard looks on their faces? The ones with slumped shoulders? They're a classic example of what we call being 'badly malled' – formerly known as 'shop till you drop', formerly formerly known as 'retail therapy'. Their bank account will be reset to zero and they'll have to attempt the climb again tomorrow.

Legend has it that the Joneses have got a mansion right at the top and they've got literally everything. Imagine how happy they must be?

But, to get to a vastly higher happiness level you have to realize that Money Mountain is a mirage. As Jamie Smart says so damned brilliantly, 'If you're caught in a trap, what's the one thing you have to do before you can escape? You have to realize that you've been caught in a trap!'[12] Ruby Wax suggests that the search for happiness is the human evolutionary equivalent of 'are we there yet?' that your kids chime from the back seat of your trip to the seaside.[13] John Naish describes it thus, 'The carrot of infinite possibilities is dangling just beyond your nose,' so wherever 'there' is, it feels like a race without a finish.'[14]

In The Land of Milk and Honey, the green grass gives you a massive clue. It isn't 'over there', it's right under your feet, so the short answer to *Are we there yet?* is *Yes we are. We always have been and we always will be. So start enjoying the view.*

There's no doubt that your brain's ability to create happiness on the horizon is a useful motivational force and we don't want you to fight the evolutionary desire to better yourself and strive for a happier future. But we don't want this drive to be happy in the future to knock you off being happy now. And, we suspect this is happening on a massive scale. Robert Holden calls it 'destination addiction',[15] a societal meme of 'Mondays are bad, Fridays are good and Wednesdays aren't too bad because it's all downhill from here' which leaves us counting down to the weekend in an accidental wishing-our-lives-away way. The sobering statistic that the average lifespan is 4000 weeks means that none of us has enough weeks left on this planet to be wishing them away.

It's your life and it's your call but, get this, I was at an event in Yorkshire a while back, doing a half-day writing workshop for 200 children. We were all seated in a big hall and the head teacher was doing a little preamble. I was perched on one of those tiny seats that you get in primary schools, sitting with a bunch of nine-year-old girls. Every time the teacher started a new sentence the little girl next to me rolled her eyes and huffed. I watched her, as predictable as a *Transformers* movie, puffing her cheeks out and harrumphing very loudly. I thought she was being rather rude so I cast a disapproving eye but she didn't stop. Every time the teacher spoke she'd shrug and sigh so in the end I leaned over and whispered, 'What on earth is wrong with you, young lady?'

She wrinkled her nose and folded her arms with a heavy sigh. 'I've just had enough,' she huffed.

'Enough of what?' I asked.

'Enough of everything, duh,' she said, as if I was an idiot, adding, 'I can't wait to retire.'

Luckily I hadn't far to fall as I spilled off my chair in shock. She's nine years old, and already counting down to retirement. This little girl is kicking her happiness into the long grass, 60 years away. As I'll be hammering throughout this book, your decision to slouch out of the house on Monday and kangaroo in on a Friday is a powerful subconscious message to those around you.

The rather unsubtle fact is that your children and grandchildren will not do what you say, but they will do what you do! It is incredibly important that you bring your happiness horizon a bit closer, in fact, as we'll see, an awful lot closer.

Will We Need Bigger Hats?

I think our minds become so cluttered with stimuli vying for our attention, we're not experiencing happy days but rather some sort of happy daze, an addled whirlwind of befuddlement. Our thinking and emotions are all over the place.

We have fallen prey to what Larry Dossey calls time-sickness: 'The belief that time is getting away ... and that you must pedal faster and faster to keep up.'[16] On this speeding treadmill, we have become hungry for information and fearful of missing out on it. So real is this fear that we've shorthanded it to FOMO. As we skim and graze, picking up one piece of entertaining information before moving onto the next in hasty bursts, we have become addicted to trivia.

What we need is some sort of mental green belt, a space for clear thinking that resists the encroaching build-up of communication.

Some people are giving it a go. I'm reliably informed that there are people resisting technology. Playfully called 'tech no's' (geddit?) they are the ones who have cut loose from the plethora of communication channels, dancing to their own, often slower tune, and possibly being more content as a result? Or they might just be left behind on the hard-shoulder of evolution while the rest of civilization speeds away? Time will tell.

But for now our children are growing up in an era where 'technology' is their first language and speed is the new intelligence. The child of the pixel and end-of-level boss – the Snapchat generation. I hear stories of children starting school unable to speak. Not mute, but they've hardly heard any language at home and have therefore not learned to communicate verbally. Neither can they use a knife and fork, but, boy, can they scoff chicken nuggets and scroll on a screen!

But I'm an oldie. My brain is already formed. I can change it a bit but there's a lot of old wiring that's been there a while and it's part of my fixtures and fittings. The current crop – generation X (factor) – have full-on 'infomaniac' tendencies that will surely be altering the structure of the human brain.

> Definition
>
> *Microwave mentality: having the attitude that if something can't be done in five minutes or less, it's not worth doing.*

I wonder whether the constant churn of trivia and their addiction to superficial information will keep young people from attending to the important issues of the day and whether their need for 'instancy' will diminish their gratitude and empathy? Will 'social media' keep them from connecting with others in a meaningful way? Will access to 'everything' enhance their happiness and wellbeing, or will they float in self-centred bubbles of solitude and befuddlement?

Or will evolution swing the other way? Access to 'all information ever', at superfast speeds, might be tremendously beneficial, propelling the human brain to new spurts of growth. Our great-great-grandchildren might be rummaging in the attic and find a chest of old clothes, our clothes, laughing at the ridiculous smallness of our hats. 'I mean, how is that ever going to fit?' they'll chuckle, sitting my baseball cap atop their extended skulls.

The heavy stuff above suggests we have neither the time nor the mental space to synthesize the information we gather and sustain it through deeper thought. So the advantage of having all the information in the world at our fingertips is lost on us unless we are able to mull it over and apply it to our lives and the important issues of our times. Otherwise it does nothing more than feed a greed for speed.

Taking time to think is not always easy. Sometimes it borders on being brave. We don't want you to live a life of unhappiness, but a little bit every now and again is good for you. Our argument boils down to this – we're living in the shallows so when we feel unhappy, we flit somewhere else to take our mind off it. We use instant stimulation as the remedy whereas sometimes a bit of contemplation might be just what we need. Instead of swimming away, stay and challenge your thinking at the next level down. We don't want you to plumb the depths (it's dangerous and dark down there) but the true answers to happiness are rarely found in the shallows.

Here's an interesting aside – I've been studying the book charts for the last few months and I can't help but notice a consistent best-selling genre in the adult non-fiction chart. And by consistent, I mean top ten for the entire year, rising to #1 for several weeks. You're curious to know, what is this best-selling genre, the books that adults have been buying in their droves?

Colouring books. *For grown-ups!* More recently, dot-to-dot books too.

The world is so frenzied that adults are finding solace in sitting at their kitchen table of an evening, tongue out and brow furrowed, trying hard to colour between the lines. I guess it's cheaper than therapy?

'Dolly Lama'

Why he was so cool ...

Mahatma Gandhi: *I think it would be a good idea.*
(When asked what he thought about Western civilization.)

Recently, I was in a plane descending into Dallas and I looked out of my porthole to see the most amazing orange sunset. This was a work trip so I was alone and the whole thing felt incomplete, as though the beauty of the moment was slipping through my fingers; almost as if this moment wasn't enough without being able to share it. It took me a second to remind myself: this moment is enough.

The point is that I needed a reminder. It's true that these moments may improve your happiness if you're able to share them, but maybe the bigger happiness prize is simply to notice and appreciate them? I'm not alone in this feeling, that the moment needs to be captured by photo to be complete, or shared on social media. It's Instagram's *raison d'etre*. Social media is clogged with pictures of what people are having for their dinner. We feel the moment isn't enough unless we talk about it, share it, capture it and somehow solidify it. It's an interesting modern phenomenon – the moment is ephemeral, and we want to ensnare it. We're like happiness lepidopterists – sticking a load of dead butterflies in a glass case is not 'happiness' but watching a red admiral flutter on a summer breeze most definitely is. You don't have to capture it, you just have to notice it.

It's become much more insidious than just posting a picture of your lunch on Instagram. We sit down to eat and feel we should be reading something online, checking messages, doing work. As if eating the food weren't enough. We take our mobile phones to the beach having a cheeky scroll while the kids are digging in the sand. Your infomaniac addiction means you're missing out on a moment – get digging! What if we accepted this present moment, and everyone and everything in it, as exactly enough? What if we needed nothing more? What if we accepted that this moment will slip away when it's done, and saw the fleeting time we had with the moment as enough, without needing to share it or capture it?

An alternative thought

'Don't just do something, sit there!' (Unknown)

Eckhart Tolle's lifetime work scrunched into a paragraph seems mightily unfair so I recommend you get your head in his book, *The Power of Now.*[17] It's fairly chunky and you might have to read it twice but the headline news is that you might be putting your happiness in the wrong time zone? My research shows that almost everyone rates their future as happier than now. I can understand that if you're unhappy now, you would naturally hope that your future might hold more happiness potential, but even chronically happy people rate their future as happier. Tolle's rather sobering thought is that the past and present can only be comprehended in this moment of thought. They don't exist anywhere else. 'Now' is all you ever have, so you may as well notice and appreciate as many moments as possible.

So having waited in the wings for an eternity, mindfulness strolls centre stage. Once again, in the interests of clarity, the shelves are groaning under the weight of mindfulness books and this is not one of them. Happiness is a several course banquet, of which mindfulness (although important) is actually just one of the flavours. It's unfair to call it 'flavour of the month' because it can be traced back to 500 BC (it's been waiting in the wings for roughly 30,000 months, even longer than Bryan Adams hung around with 'Everything I do, I do it for you'). So rather than 'new', we think it's safe to say that mindfulness is experiencing a resurgence. More aptly, maybe a rebirth? Whatever: this quiet, Eastern unlit corner of happiness has been thrust into the Western glare. So, shining a light into its eyes and demanding who and what it is, what would we find?

As we've learned in other lands (and on Money Mountain in particular), the Western way is one of accumulation and attachment. Indeed, you have spent your entire life learning how to be unhappy! We pin our happiness onto things and people and we become terribly upset when those things or people disappear.

In the broadest of Eastern philosophy, there are two stand-out points. Firstly, nothing is permanent. Being happy is often a matter of learning new ways of thinking but more often it's about letting go of the old ways. So, in a reversal of thinking, mindfulness is less about holding on and much more about letting go. If nothing is permanent, then it makes sense to enjoy it while it's here and let it go when its time has passed. So simply 'experiencing' without 'attaching' is part of the deal.

Nice theory, but letting go of attachments presents a huge challenge. It goes against societal norms. Look around and you'll see people musterbating like mad. Go on, admit it, you are a musterbator. I know I am. Perhaps I'd better explain? Musterbation is the elevation of things we'd like to have into things we believe we MUST have. No wonder we're all so bleary eyed. Think back to ten years ago, and all those things you wanted – nice house, decent education, kids, new kitchen, half-decent job, two holidays a year, a better car, gym membership, new sofa ... and today, you have all those things. You've done it! I hardly dare ask, are you any happier?

I asked the Doctor whether masturbation causes poor eyesight.

He said, 'You're in Sainsbury's, mate!'

The happiness model is flawed. According to James Wall-man, we are evolutionarily programmed to cling to stuff. In times of scarcity, this desire for material goods had a real survival benefit but in the current age of abundance, this evolutionary hangover is causing us all to drown in our own glut. His book describes how our hoarding tendencies are clogging up our lives. The solution, according to Wallman, is to spend our money on experiences (like concerts, holidays and education) and less on stuff. Or, let me clarify, if you want to buy things you're better off avoiding designer cloth-ing, jewellery and artwork, and investing in snowboards, climbing gear and bicycles. As Wallman says, 'You can't have the experiences without the stuff.'[18]

But rest assured, if you were expecting some sort of whimsical Eastern words of wisdom that money is the root of all evil, let the shrill voice inside your head subside; yes, relax, shopping will make you happy. But 'stuff' will only get you a short-term fix, so to squeeze more value from your happiness pound, you're better off buying an experience.

Let's have a go at applying mindfulness to the Western world. Our entire economy is founded on human weakness – hair salons, sports cars, fast food, shoe shops, travel agents, plastic surgeons – self-doubt and dissatisfaction draw us into purchases to fill the void with a short-term fix. These are the things we climb Money Mountain to obtain.

Retail therapy is like taking an antacid tablet for indiges-tion. The antacid will coat your stomach and take away the burning, leaving you free to stuff your face with more curry.

Likewise, buying things calms and soothes the immediate fury of unease but it won't create long-term contentment.

Chris Barez-Brown nails this with: 'Mindfulness is simply being aware of what is happening right now without wishing it were different; enjoying the pleasant without holding onto it when it changes (which it will); being with the unpleasant without fearing it will always be this way (which it won't).'[19]

Mindfulness, for me, is a challenge. I can't sit, doing nothing, focusing on my breathing, contemplating my 'now'. I know that hard-core Buddhists will be shouting at me (I get a strange satisfaction from making Buddhists angry) when I tell them I haven't got time to meditate. I've got things to do; a dishwasher to unload, some emails to check and a book to write (and, no, almost certainly not in that order). I fall in line with (Buddhist) Michael Foley who gave age-old relaxation techniques a good go before reflecting that the present moment is kind of overrated. I mean, seriously – what's the big deal? Breathe in, breathe out. After doing it like billions of times, I kind of know the drill. Yeah, I'm glad those lungs of mine are still working. It's just not super-exciting to focus on ALL the freaking time.'[20]

And here's a delicious Mickey-take of the whole 'mindfulness for business people' band-wagon in which large corporations and schools are sourcing mindfulness programmes for stressed out staff and kids. After a session with 'Dolly Lama', one formerly disgruntled employee was clearly won over. 'I thought I hated my job, and it turns out I've been experiencing nirvana! Who knew?' He patted his ample belly and added, 'Plus, the fat Buddha statue in the conference room makes me feel better about my gut.'

On a deadly serious note, rather than providing Indian head massages for stressed-out employees, would it not be more sensible to simply stop working them to death in the first place?

What I can do is appreciate what Robert Holden calls 'the beautiful ordinary'.[21] If mindfulness is telling us to savour the moments, then we must start to notice joy and abundance in the smallest things. If we're to truly quit waiting, cease comparing, stop chasing, and open ourselves up to the possibility that happiness is here, now, we have to get good at spotting it. The beautiful ordinary says it's everywhere and in almost everything. The opportunities for taking in the good are multitudinal, but while the bad is heralded with a trumpet fanfare, the good is often silently sitting at the back of your awareness. For me, mindfulness is less about donning rose-tinted specs and more about cleaning the shit off your current ones. Plus, by taking in the good, you learn to feel a whole lot better – more vital – and are therefore better able to deal with the bad.

The best thing about mindfulness is that after a while you realize it's all transient. And by 'it' I mean 'absolutely everything'. So don't feel compelled to grab onto the good moments and snuggle your face into them, crying your heart out when they disappear. There is more good on the way. Good is in every moment.

All this knowledge and experience doesn't make you immune from struggle. The same bad stuff will still happen to you but arming yourself with a bit of inner wisdom does offer respite and the ability to move ahead without having to pull a wagon load of baggage from the past with you. This was said a whole lot more eloquently by David Pollay[22] whose 'Law of the Garbage Truck' made it into our previous book but it's so beautiful that it bears repeating ...

I hopped in a taxi, and we took off for Grand Central Station. We were driving in the right lane when all of a sudden, a black car jumped out of a parking space right in front of us. My taxi driver slammed on his brakes, the car skidded, the tires squealed, and at the very last moment our car stopped just one inch from the other car's back-end.

I couldn't believe it. But then I couldn't believe what happened next. The driver of the other car, the guy who almost caused a big accident, whipped his head around and he started yelling bad words at us. And for emphasis, he threw in a one finger salute, as if his words were not enough.

But then here's what really blew me away. My taxi driver just smiled and waved at the guy. And I mean, he was friendly. So, I said, 'Why did you just do that? This guy could have killed us!'

And this is when my taxi driver told me what I now call 'The Law of the Garbage Truck'. He said, 'Many people are like garbage trucks. They run around full of garbage, full of frustration, full of anger, and full of disappointment. As their garbage piles up, they look for a place to dump it. And if you let them, they'll dump it on you. So when someone wants to dump on you, don't take it personally. Just smile, wave, wish them well, and move on. Believe me. You'll be happier.'

So I started thinking, how often do I let Garbage Trucks run right over me? And how often do I take their garbage and spread it to other people at work, at home, or on the street? It was then that I said, 'I don't want their garbage and I'm not going to spread it anymore.'

Gratitude

Meet mindfulness's hipster friend, gratitude. They've been #besties, like forevs. In fact, they're inseparable.

Before we talk about gratitude, here's an important but technical point about happiness. No matter how incredible a moment is, you can't force someone to experience its 'incredibleness' and no matter how happy you are, you can't give someone your happiness.

Happiness is part of your healthy functioning and like the rest of your health, it can't be shared. Sure, you can lead by example and you can most certainly influence people (in fact you cannot NOT influence people, as we'll see later) but you can't strap people down and command positive thoughts or beat happiness into them (well, actually, you can do that, but it won't have the desired effect).

So, your happiness is totally selfish. It's 100 per cent about you. The trick is to transmit happiness to others on the understanding that there's no guarantee they'll catch it.

If you reverse the trick, it's equally important to be immune from other people's negativity. Once again, easier said than done because you're wired to connect. The majority of folk spend an inordinate amount of time grumbling about what they haven't got. You don't have to be 'most people'. So flip your thinking and spend an inordinate amount of time being grateful for what you have got. The posh word for this is 'gratitude' and you can get started right now by listing 20 things that you really appreciate but take for granted. The first few are easy, then you'll get stuck and weird things will creep in. Have a look at your list and magnetic it to your fridge so you can see it every day. I think you'll find you're luckier than you ever imagined.

> Nod off with a smile
>
> *Having trouble sleeping? Try counting your blessings.*

So, if happiness is part of your healthy functioning, and mindfulness is a way of noticing, gratitude is what helps keep your internal boiler stoked. This all makes perfect sense until you listen to John Naish describe our bombardment of information like dolphin sonar.[23] The cruelty of captivity means their sonar bounces around, deafening and confusing the poor creatures, and it's a bit like that in our world of infomania – we become deafened by messages bouncing around, snagging our attention.

It's pretty much a first for the human species. For the vast majority of time that humans have occupied the planet we haven't had enough food, warmth or shelter and life was, I would imagine, rather grim. Indeed, we forget that many countries are exactly like that. Now we have it all and we're in danger of overshooting the runway in a quest to obtain just a little more than we actually need.

Gratitude helps us put the brakes on (either a little or a lot, it's up to you) and it's something that you can practice. Do it every morning when you wake up (*woohoo, I'm alive*), while you brush your teeth (*how amazing, I still have my own teeth*), look in the mirror (*hello gorgeous*), sit on the loo (*oh, what a feeling!*) and think of five things you're grateful for (*sit-down toilets, sewage systems, not being constipated, soft loo roll and running water*).

You'll be grinning your way out of the bathroom because gratitude acts like fertilizer for happiness.

Septic Sceptics

Miguel Farias and Catherine Wikholm add a healthy spoonful of scepticism to proceedings, daring to look at mindfulness with a critical eye. In *The Buddha Pill* they suggest that in our modern culture, everyone is looking for some 'hack' or shortcut to wellbeing, with mindfulness and meditation deemed to be the latest prescription.[24]

Maybe?

Nobody can tell for sure whether mindfulness will be around in, say, 100 years? But seeing as it's managed to hang in there for 3500 years, we're fairly sure it will be there or thereabouts. Let's leave the last paragraph in The Land of Milk and Honey to the philosopher Alain de Botton,[25] another sceptic, but in a clever way. De Botton suggests that, in centuries past, people knew where they fitted into the social order. If you were born a peasant, you knew you were a peasant. If you were born a Lord, you knew you were a Lord. There was no mobility or opportunity, and so there was no stress about getting ahead. You weren't responsible for your birthright, so you accepted it and lived up (or down) to it. Google the Indian caste system if you want a modern day equivalent.

It's easy to argue against this but if we assume for a minute that Britain is a 'meritocracy' (defined as 'everyone with skill and imagination may aspire to reach the highest level') then the rules suddenly change. In a meritocracy, if you're poor and you work hard to get an education, start a business and rise to the top, it's not an accident. The mantra of a meritocracy is that anyone can achieve anything they want, with a dollop of hard work, a bit of luck and a following wind. The 'merit' bit means you've earned it.

But the success coin also has a reverse side. If you stay at the bottom of the pile or if you rise to the top and lose it all again, it's your fault. You're the failure. You're the one who never made anything of your life or, indeed, who lost everything. And this causes people to live shackled with a constant fear of inadequacy. Nobody ever wins. If you earn success, you're petrified that it might not last. If you don't experience success you worry that you're a failure and, tellingly, you can end up resenting those who do succeed.

Top Tip (and a challenge) ...

Try Shonette's list of 20 things to do before you're 9¾...

1. Go on a treasure hunt.
2. Make bread from scratch.
3. Stroke a rabbit.
4. Build a den under the table.
5. Roll down a grassy hill.
6. Catch raindrops on your tongue.
7. Ditto snow.
8. Play hopscotch.
9. Catch a crab in a bucket.
10. Play Pooh sticks.
11. Have unlimited toppings on your ice-cream.
12. Join a Guinness World Record attempt.
13. Visit a pick-your-own farm.
14. Make a sock puppet and do a show.

15. Do a coin rubbing.

16. Toast marshmallows.

17. Slide full body on a muddy field.

18. Fly a kite.

19. Eat an apple straight from the tree.

20. Camp in the wild.

Our challenge is this: *how many can you tick off this week?*

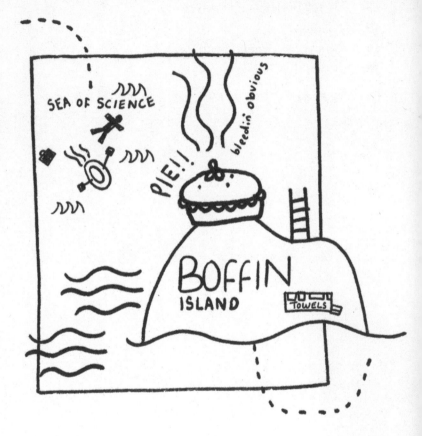

Chapter 6
BOFFIN ISLAND

• • • • • •

In which we clamber ashore and towel ourselves dry.

Boffin Island is a real bastard to get to, accessible by dinghy across the mountainous waves of the Sea of Science. It's hard to tell how many people have set sail and never made it.

But we're here, so what can we expect? Well, how about we explore the different types of 'psychology' before homing in on the super-sexy drop-dead-gorgeous smiley type. Then we learn a little about being a researcher before Andy tells you all about his PhD. No really, don't glaze over, it's very interesting stuff presented as only he can – as a card game and a pie.

Then we tell you a whole load of stuff that you already know, like how pain makes you happy, how attitudinal choice is like your eyelashes and why trying to be happy might make you unhappy. Then it's off down to the allotment followed by a bit of 'life-crafting', before we come back to the recurring happiness theme of Boffin Island – PIE!

Not that you'll be feeling like eating pie after that perilous sea crossing. It's almost like those waves are deliberately whipped up to stop people travelling?

Boffin Island is a lovely place btw. Best not to chat to the locals though, it's not exactly a foreign language, just Double Dutch. Oh, and before we begin our tour please excuse the smell – it's a continual whiff of the bleedin' obvious.

Enjoy!

••••••

FARGIN (YIDDISH): TO GLOW WITH PRIDE AT THE SUCCESS OF OTHERS.

••••••

Happiness Catwalk

Heavy academia is analogous to a fashion show. You see the outrageous catwalk outfits and think *#wtf? How can anyone wear that?* And then it gets watered down, simplified and interpreted into something that appears in the high street. Something that started off as unthinkable and unpalatable gets translated for the masses.

I didn't realize until recently that research has the same premise? I've come across reams of meaningless academic twaddle that doesn't look good at all. But sometimes, if you can adapt it, interpret it and translate it, there are messages that are good for mass consumption.

I guess that's an admission that I'm not the Jean Paul Gautier of happiness. I'm a bit more Top Shop?

I studied at university many years ago. I struggled with 'statistics' and found 'economic principles' pretty heavy going too. On the flip side, I found 'psychology' astoundingly interesting. We read reassuringly weighty textbooks about phobias, disorders, anxiety and depression and I got proper stuck into the dark side of human nature and became conversant with suffering in all its misshapen human forms.

I revelled in the science of misery because, at that time, psychology was almost exclusively about 'what could go wrong with you'. As a psychologist, you'd be trained to provide therapeutic or chemical remedies ... giving you a proper pants-on-the-outside job of saving those who needed saving.

The underlying assumption of traditional strands of psychology was – and largely still is – about people who are struggling. There's clinical psychology (for individuals with mental health issues), community psychology (for groups of people with mental health problems), child psychology (does what it says on the tin), forensic psychology (working with offenders and the justice system), health psychology (helping people to stop smoking, drinking...), occupational psychology (largely concerned with how you assess people prior to interview so you don't recruit too many psychopaths), consumer psychologists (how to get you to buy things you don't want), and, increasingly, geropsychology (mostly about reducing loneliness and depression amongst old people). There are more, but you get my drift. The raging river of psychology is being fed by a myriad of specialist tributaries.

Please note, my pen-portraits aren't meant in derogatory terms. These branches of psychology are astonishingly important and, I might add, life changing. However, it's interesting to reflect on my time at university, studying to degree and masters' levels, that there was never a single lecture on happiness. We'd spend a semester looking at eating disorders, and zero minutes examining people who didn't have eating disorders. Ditto, depression versus flourishing, anxiety versus confidence and misery versus happiness.

These latter subjects didn't exist as worthy subjects because, of course, the people aren't ill. They don't need 'fixing'. I don't think that the merest notion of having lectures on 'flourishing', 'confidence', 'strengths' and 'happiness' had even flickered across the awareness of the psychological community. It had certainly never crossed my mind to raise my hand in a packed lecture theatre and ask, 'This stuff on disorders is really interesting Prof, but why can't we study people are feeling amazing, find out what they're doing and maybe share some of that? Would that learning not help those who are struggling?'

Yes, positive psychology was a proper Rumsfeldian 'unknown unknown'. When you're 96 and you look back at your primary school photos, there will be one classmate who you can't name. For hundreds of years, positive psychology was that kid. It was there all along, but nobody actually noticed. Until, along came the grand-pappy of positive psychology, the esteemed Prof Marty Seligman, he to whom we must doff our happiness caps. He moved the polite and hitherto quiet kid to the front of the class. Not only did the quiet kid find its voice, it grew into an unruly ADHD teenager and has been kicking off ever since.

During his tenure as president of the American Psychological Association, Seligman planted the psychology of human flourishing centre stage, which, to be fair, was a very bold thing to do. He must have put a lot of academic noses out of joint. People who had made 50-year careers out of exploring the darkest depths of the murky world of depression were suddenly confronted with the sunlit shallows of flourishing, a coral reef of science exploding with colour and aliveness.

A few deep breaths and 'positive psychology' finally found its confidence and its voice. It has since grown into a formidable science of all things flourishing, its gorgeousness attracting a swathe of academic interest. I don't want a divorce from 'normal psychology', I mean, we've been together for a very long time. But I have to say, I quite fancy her younger sister. She smiles more.

The Art of Complexity

So, a quick word about the system. Young and naïve, I started out on the PhD journey and learned a similar lesson to The Clash. In their case they fought the law and the law won – in my case, I fought the academic system and the academic system won. Yes, I agree, it's not as catchy as the original, but an almost exact reflection of my naïvety. My aim was to rebel against what I perceived to be an impenetrable academic jungle and produce a thesis that was written in plain simple English – something that would be accessible to non-academics, like myself. Twelve years later, the system had clubbed me into submission and, fair play to it, grudgingly, it has won me over. If people are to trust academia, and indeed, if it informs decision making, it needs to be based on solid foundations.

My PhD investigated happiness and flourishing in the workplace so, basically, for ten years I sought out happy people and followed them around to try and find out why they were so happy. The basic premise is that you have to study something to geek level (that's the level just above 'nerd') which adds to the body of knowledge that is already out there. I get what Isaac Newton meant when he said 'If I have seen further it is by standing on the shoulders of giants'.

So, to business. 'Languishing' is a term I hate. A quick Google dictionary search finds the definition to be 'lose or lack vitality, waste away, rot, decay, wither, be abandoned, be neglected, be forgotten, suffer'. Yuk! But this term isn't solely for negative or vacant people. Some folk can have a good job, a nice family life and still end up feeling empty or lost on the inside. So I decided to explore the opposite of languishing, which, for the purposes of this book, I will call 'flourishing'. The same lazy Google dictionary search shows it defined as 'grow, thrive, prosper, do well, develop, burgeon, increase' as well as 'to attract attention' (as in 'the referee flourished a red card'). And that last bit is crucial because it was one of the levels through which I sieved my PhD candidates.

Bear with me, this is a technical but important point. One of the reasons my doctorate took so long is that I spent two years collecting the wrong data. I'd approach an organization and do a staff survey where people rated their happiness on a scale of 1–10. With the notion of simplicity at the forefront of my mind, I would then follow up by interviewing those who scored 8 or above. They were statistically well above the happiness average so who were they and what were their secrets? Two years later I'd discovered that a lot of them were deluded, irritating, faking it or so excruciatingly off the grid of normality that they scared me. There's a very good reason why Tigger hasn't got any friends!

So I started again and this time I changed the focus from 'self-rated happiness' towards 'flourishing' which, put simply, is when your good feelings leak out of you and infect others; a bit like an emotional virus, but in a good way. I like to think of flourishing as an 'outbreak' of happiness?

So, I raised the bar. In order to attract my academic interest you now had to jump through three hoops. Hoop one, same as before, you had to rate as 8 or above on self-rated 'happiness' and 'energy'. Hoop two, you had to score in the upper quartile of a recognized, tried-and-tested happiness questionnaire. And hoop three, the clincher, you had to be mentioned at least three times by other people in the organization as 'someone at work who makes me feel good'. While I appreciate the hardened academics will still be able to find ample fault with this methodology, it started getting me access to the right kind of people. It sharpened the data and, best of all, filtered out the happiness weirdos!

Ten-Card Shuffle

Academia is a never-ending game of one-upmanship. Researchers spend a long time 'proving' something and then the rest of the academic community picks it to pieces. Let's take the 50/10/40 happiness ratio, which has been proved and disproved several times over. Sonia Lyubomirsky puts it in an easy-peasy pie-chart,[26] and we three love pies.

What Determines Happiness?

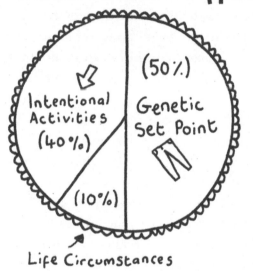

Life Circumstances

Taking the big wedge first, it seems that 50 per cent of your total happiness is down to your genes, so if you've got smiley parents you have a good baseline. The word on the academic street is that you can't do much about this portion of your happiness – it's fixed.

Examining the skinny 'life circumstances' portion of the happiness pie, evidence suggests that 10 per cent of an individual's happiness is determined by factors that constitute the background of their life. If these heavyweight academics (huge brains, not necessarily huge bodies) are to be believed, the totality of your circumstances (e.g. gender, ethnicity, traumas, triumphs, marital status, education level, health, income, physical appearance and your lifestyle) accounts for only 10 per cent of your happiness pie. This counter-intuitivity is hard to believe to the point that Lyubomirsky herself has to go to great lengths to hammer it home: 'The general conclusion from almost a century of research on the determinants of wellbeing is that objective circumstances, demographic variables and life events are correlated with happiness less strongly than intuition and every day experience tell us they ought to be.'[27]

The point is that you can influence this section of the pie, but only in the medium to long term. There is evidence that subjective wellbeing is, on average, higher among those who are married, participate in religious and leisure activities, earn more money, are of higher social and occupational status, view themselves as healthy and live in prosperous, democratic countries. Others have shown that individuals are likely to become happier if a close friend or neighbour has become happier in the preceding six months, pointing to the contagious nature of emotions as an open loop. Common sense tells us that immediate situational occurrences are important in explaining variance in happiness. For example, research on 'hassles' and 'uplifts' identified a host of minor daily events that result in negative and positive emotions, respectively. In the workplace, the 'hassles' included meetings and negative colleagues while the 'uplifts' included achievements and interacting with positive colleagues.

So, the story so far is that 50 per cent of your happiness is fixed by your genes and a further 10 per cent by your circumstances. Later, I will venture to disagree with the boffins who suggest that neither of these portions of the pie are malleable in the immediacy of the moment. But for now, I'll keep the peace and go with the suggestion that the remaining 40 per cent of an individual's happiness – the 'intentional activities' section of the pie – is directly under our control. According to Lyubomirsky, 'intentional activities' include an array of techniques including practising gratitude, kindness, forgiveness, spirituality, choosing and pursuing authentic goals, nurturing social relationships, seeking opportunities to experience flow and engaging in meditation and physical exercise.

It is this sizeable chunk of happiness that gives us scope to raise our levels in the here and now. If you'll allow me to analogize the happiness pie to a card game – let's call it 'ten-card shuffle'. The game starts with the hand of fate dealing five cards to everyone on the planet. These cards represent your genetic make-up, they make up half your hand, and they're fixed. Then, a bit later in the game, you get another card – representing your circumstances – which you have to keep in your hand for a while but can change eventually. Crucially, there are four more cards that make up your hand. Most people just accept the cards that the croupier deals them but the truth is that you can actually choose these cards. Best of all, you can swap these cards instantly, and as often as you like.

Your genes hand you a starting point but everything else in the game is up for grabs. You can shape your circumstances and your attitudinal choice is entirely down to you. You can create a winning hand and most importantly, how you play your hand is up to you.

Back to my findings. My respondents were registering 23 per cent happier than the person sitting next to them in the office. As well as being significantly happier, my research subjects also recorded 24 per cent higher energy levels than their counterparts.

> *I wish I was a glow worm, a glow worm's never glum, cos how can you be grumpy, when the sun shines out your bum.*
>
> The glow worm song

Imagine cranking up your happiness and energy by nearly a quarter? What would you look, sound and feel like? I'm imagining a very smiley, invigorated, sparkly, joyous, enthusiastic version of you? But there's a problem in being that person. Psychologists have identified an obstacle to change: the 'genetic set point', a kind of default setting or equilibrium state of self which Schopenhauer defines as 'our primary and inborn character' – the 50 per cent piece of pie.

But the other 50 per cent of the pie gives us hope. 'Life Circumstances' and 'Intentional Activities' are ours for the changing. What if the 'set point' isn't in fact set, but just 'familiar'? And that we could become 'familiar' with happiness at a higher level?

The short answer is we can, and it's deadly simple, but not very easy.

No Pain, No Gain?

So 40 per cent of your happiness is accounted for by 'intentional activities' – it's down to you, right here, right now.

It may well take some effort to rethink how you think and to inhabit a world of positive mental habits. If you want to be world class at anything, there's a serious amount of effort involved. The current thinking is that 10,000 hours is what's required to be awesome (another 'fact' that has been proved and disproved a dozen times). So to become a fabulous chef, a half decent footballer, a competent vet, or a karate black belt – these things don't happen by accident.

Flourishing is exactly the same. The first rule of happy club is that you have to be committed to commitment. Interestingly, I recently received an email from a lady who had attended one of my workshops, loved it, went away and did it, and reported that she was exhausted from being happy! I told her that the commitment to flourishing requires that you go beyond the bump in the road. And the bend. And up the mountain path. If it was a bike ride your thighs would be screaming in pain. But the metaphors got tangled so I deleted it and suggested she tried being miserable for a week and got back to me with a couple of paragraphs of 'compare and contrast'. Perhaps she was disarmed by my apparent flippancy (which I didn't mean) but she never did get back to me.

Training yourself to be a mental ninja of happiness requires effort. In my experience, lots of it! The payback, over your lifetime, is incalculable. The problem is that you might already have spent 10,000 hours learning to settle into a mediocre bog-standard level of happiness. 'Making do' or 'getting by' with a default attitude that fits in with everyone else – otherwise known as mediocrity.

Just to add to your burden, 10,000 hours of practising to be your best self isn't always a guarantee. As Paul McCartney once pointed out, there are loads of bands out there who practise for more than 10,000 hours, most of whom never make it. Life can be akin to a pavement of sticky dog turds. Sometimes, no matter how positive you are, you're going to step in something rather nasty.

I figure that you can teach people the principles of positive psychology in three hours flat. But you can't, not in a lifetime, teach them to keep applying the principles. That comes from within. My PhD respondents haven't bolted positivity onto their lives, they've integrated the principles so they become part of their life. That requires a big dollop of something that, in a fast-paced now-now-now society is in short supply; namely, commitment.

You see the science of happiness is so obvious that we miss it. The choice to be positive is like your eyelashes: with you in every moment, part of you, everywhere you look, yet never seen. And to take you a little deeper into the strangulating undergrowth of the happiness jungle, this choice thing doesn't work the other way. Nobody chooses to be miserable, grumpy or angry. Nobody slumps out of bed with the internal dialogue of, 'I'm determined to have a real stinker today' (I appreciate that it might seem that way, but I promise you it isn't). My research shows very clearly that with 'choice' comes 'effort'.

To make the point, have a go at making sense of these weird real-life contradictions if you can:

- I recently completed a half marathon. I don't really like running. I find it boring and it gives me shin splints.
- My kids have just left or are about to leave home. Parenting, particularly in the early days, was exhausting. My kids didn't come with a user manual and I often got frustrated at my parental cack-handedness.
- I run a training company that often requires me to work 80 hours a week.
- I travel a lot. I don't like working such long hours and I have grown to dislike motorways and budget hotel chains.
- I write books that have such tight deadlines that I sometimes have to stay up until 2am to finish chapters. I don't like staying up past 10pm. It's a chore.

All of these activities have ingredients that I find exceedingly unpleasant. They all require me to set my personal bar ridiculously high to the point that I will sometimes fail. Yet, they are some of the most meaningful moments and activities of my life. They involve pain, effort, struggle, even anger and despair, yet once completed, I look back and get misty-eyed about them.

Why? Because it's these sorts of activities that give me purpose. It's the perpetual pursuit of fulfilling our ideal selves which grants us happiness, regardless of superficial pleasures or pain, regardless of positive or negative emotions. I'd venture that the end results don't define our ideal selves. It's not finishing the half marathon that makes me happy, it's achieving a difficult long-term goal. It's not the business profits that make me happy, it's the process of overcoming all the odds with people I care about. It's not having awesome kids that makes me happy, but knowing that I gave myself up to the growth of another human being that is special. And, to be fair, my wife mucked in as and when.

Big, important sentence alert! The effort of trying to be happy runs the serious risk of making you unhappy. Because to 'try' to be happy implies that you are not already inhabiting your ideal self, you are not aligned with the qualities of who you wish to be. After all, if you were acting out your ideal self, then you wouldn't feel the need to try to be happy.

A more interesting question that perhaps you've never considered before is what pain do you want in your life? Or maybe, what are you willing to struggle for? Everybody

wants to have great qualifications, an amazing job and financial independence but not everyone wants to suffer through
60-hour work weeks, long commutes, two evenings a week at
night school or to remain positive while inhabiting the blasé
confines of an infinite corporate hell.

Bottom line? There is significant mental effort in being
your best self. It's a commitment to a way of thinking that
you have to do every day for the rest of your life. You never
'arrive' at the perfect sculpted mind and, unfortunately, if
you have a month off, the bad habits will grow back.

Here's the truth. Being a positive, effervescent, inspired
human being is hard work. But it's not half as exhausting as
being miserable.

Technicalities

Here's another technicality. It's not a choice to be happy, it's
a choice to be as positive as life will allow you. Remember,
from The Land of Marshmallows and Unicorns, you cannot
command happiness, but you can allow it. Happiness is less
of an outcome and more *something you have to open up to.*

Consciously and deliberately choosing to be positive puts
you in a better place (emotionally), which triggers more
optimism, hence you can see solutions and have a better
chance of feeling happy. While the conscious and deliberate
'choice to be positive' seems intuitively obvious, I promise
you that the vast majority of people are failing to exercise it.
So, what if you spent the same amount of time working on

your attitude as you did on choosing your breakfast cereal? I've just checked online and there are 390 choices of cereal. What if there are also 390 choices of attitude? In fact, you could make a list, right now – a shopping list of attitudes, all available to you right now: happy, upbeat, sad, grumpy, elated, pleased, grateful, obnoxious, impatient, awesome, energetic, lethargic, buoyant, joyous, confident, miserable, ungrateful, jealous, spiteful, lethargic, buzzing ... these, and a whole lot more, are available to you.

Obviously, some of these feelings will work better than others. Having studied happy people for the best part of ten years, you're better off doing what my research group do, and learning to craft an attitude that is beneficial to your wellbeing. Instead of leafing through the catalogue of life focusing on material possessions, you'd be better off browsing the 'emotional states' pages and choosing a few corking attitudes.

Stopping for a breather...

So, let's bring a few chapters together for a second.

In Zombie Land we learned that Mondays are bad and Fridays good, right? And in Travel Planning we suggested that wearing your best undergarments makes you feel good. In the Meadows of Marshmallows and Unicorns we found that chocolate, sex and alcohol are hedonistic routes to instant happiness.

A University of Bristol study reports that the key to long-term happiness is, erm, gardening?[28]

So here's a top mind-blowing happiness overload, on Friday night why not don your best knickers and take the person you love with a bottle of red and a slab of Cadbury's Dairy Milk, down to the allotment...

Or is that too much happiness, even for you?

It's All About Positive Thinking, Right?

Erm, wrong!

Positive psychology focuses on positive aspects of well-being including (but not limited to) positive emotions, happiness, hope, optimism and other constructs that relate to the idea of positive thinking. To the uninformed, it would be easy to assume that positive psychology and positive thinking are strongly related. Some might even say, *Finally, science is proving what we have always thought to be true about positive thinking.* But while positive thinking and positive psychology may be related, they are more like third cousins than twin sisters.

Positive psychology begins with scientific inquiry so takes some of those assumptions about positive thinking and says, *let's test them to see where they hold true.* Positive thinking encourages an optimistic outlook even when one isn't warranted by the situation, so for example, proponents will suggest 'affirmations', advocating that you should stand in front of the mirror and chant 'I am a millionaire' when patently, you're not. Psychology researchers don't generally advocate lying to yourself or promoting uninhibited optimism in all situations. As Martin Seligman says, 'you don't want the pilot who is de-icing the wings of your plane to be an optimist'.[29]

Acacia Parks suggests that the positive psychology brand of optimism is not about being positive all the time but about 'entertaining the possibility that things could work out', something that might best be described as 'realistic optimism'.[30] In this respect, the benefit of optimism comes from being open to it, not from blindly following it even when it makes no sense to do so.

······

'I'M CONSTANTLY AMAZED AT HOW DIFFERENT MY TWIN DAUGHTERS ARE. LISA IS SO MUCH MORE POSITIVE AND CONFIDENT THAN HER SISTER HOG FACE.'

······

Danny Zuker

Your brain is astoundingly sophisticated yet supremely stupid. For example, your brain is very poor at distinguishing between what's really happening and what you are merely imagining. Which is why sad films make you blub, horror films make your neck hairs stand up and porn films, *err...*

ahem, well you know what I mean. We see the images and our brain interprets them as real, thus activating the necessary flood of emotions. And your emotions cause physical reactions. Imagine if you spoke to your friends in the same way that the voice in your head speaks to you? No friends left! Positive psychology says it's time to be your own best friend.

Simple Simon

So, rearranging your mental habits – aka 'choosing to be positive' – involves a series of smaller actions that also fall into the 'simple but not easy' category. My research suggests that happy people engage in positive pep talks as well as reframing negative events, thereby giving life a positive spin.

They also engage in a host of other feats of positive mental agility, including setting rather large and exciting personal goals, playing to their strengths and being grateful. They also attack, with some gusto, the 10 per cent of the happiness pie (circumstances) that other researchers suggest is fixed. They engage in what I call 'life-crafting', otherwise known as 'taking personal responsibility' for their happiness. So, for example, while a lot of people will endure a miserable working life, my flourishing respondents will give it a good shot but if they can't feel great they will find another job. Once again, it has a whiff of the bleedin' obvious about it, but daring to up sticks and move on involves a bit of a risk. I once had a delegate on a course who said (devoid of humour or irony): 'I've worked here 29 years and haven't had a good day yet.' My PhD respondents simply wouldn't settle for that. Their brains work in the opposite direction to most so while the neg-heads endure a life of corporate hell (thinking it's not my dream job but it's too risky to leave) the happy ones clear their desk and move on (figuring life is a short and precious gift and it's too risky to be unhappy and stay).

If you're unhappy, is the 'risk' greater in staying or in leaving? I describe it in my thesis as the classic Herbert Simon economic argument between 'satisficing' and 'maximizing'.[31] Most people find an attitude that's 'fine'. They make do. My flourishing people are seeking to maximize their attitudinal choices, which means they are continually searching for an optimum rather than making do with standard. This shift to attitudinal maximizing works in their favour, creating more energy, positivity and opportunity.

Thinking inside the box...

True (and very sad) story.

A charity fought for the release of a circus bear. Beatriz was an eight-year-old brown bear who had been trained to dance for the Russian public. She was well travelled, secured in her 12-foot cage.

After securing her release the charity team took her to the forest and opened her cage door.

> *Beatriz was enticed out into the vast wilderness of the Ural Mountains and spent her time pacing an area of ground measuring 12 feet by 12 feet.*
>
> *And we can't help thinking, there's a powerful message in there somewhere?*

And so to our final lesson from Boffin Island. Emotions, as consensus generally says, are triggered by thoughts, and thoughts happen in your head. Yet we talk about 'gut instinct', a call-to-action that stems from a feeling somewhere in the pit of your stomach. At several times in your life you will have had 'butterflies' in your tummy or been 'sick to your stomach'. That's because your gut is lined with 100 million neurons. The 'enteric brain' (as it is sometimes called) is connected to the central nervous system via the vagus nerve so, despite everything being connected, your gut can also operate completely independently of your brain. It turns out that the brain in your tummy is in charge of an awful lot of very important things; it majors in the release of serotonin (an antidepressant chemical) as well as playing a crucial role in the way we experience emotion.

But the story gets curiouser and curiouser. It seems that 90 per cent of nerve fibres are dedicated to transmitting information upwards towards the brain so there is an information superhighway going north, gut to brain. The road south is much narrower, carrying just 10 percent of the traffic. Therefore your enteric brain may play an enormous role in what you experience mentally, but the brain in your head has little control over your gut instinct.

So, our hunch has been right all along. Happiness is in your head but also in your stomach, hence why 'happiness pie' makes perfect sense.

Top Tips

1. Learn a happiness lesson from the happiest person you know. Who is it? Why do you think they're happy?
2. Play ten-card shuffle wisely. Remember, swapping your cards is not cheating, it's in the rules (indeed, you are cheating yourself if you don't swap them).
3. Be committed to positivity. It takes effort to be your best self.
4. Find your purpose (*what do you stand for/what are you all about?* in one sentence).
5. Stop trying to be happy and 'open up to happiness'.

6. Stop making do with mediocre attitudes and become an attitude maximizer.

7. Change your default chatter from 'what's the worst that could happen?' to 'what's the best that could happen?'

Chapter 7

THE PROMISED LAND

• • • • • •

In which we scramble across some stony ground before ascending up, up, to Cloud 9 and beyond.

Here we examine why happiness was invented, throwing a few benefits into the mix. It's no wonder happiness is the ONE thing you wish for your offspring. After proposing happiness might be a relatively modern evolutionary bolt-on, we rewind to a much bigger question with God in one corner and Mr Darwin in the other. We don't want to offend so take the cowardly way and look at it through the eyes of Harold, Daisy and the blobfish (yes, dear reader, those words have never appeared together in any language) before expanding a single blobfish into 'Blob Theory'. That's when Andy C gets a breather, leaving you in the trembling hands and with the bloodied forehead of Andy W.

The chapter finishes with 'Ten (Tweetable) Happiness Commandments', updated for the modern world.

Welcome to the Promised Land. Technically speaking it's only really available after you've died, but in a rare opportunity, we have some backstage passes.

Please keep to the guided path – there are no trespassers.

Eyes wide shut, off we go …

• • • • • •

ULTRACREPIDARIANISM (ENGLISH, BUT ONLY JUST): THE HABIT OF GIVING OPINIONS AND ADVICE OUTSIDE OF ONE'S KNOWLEDGE OR COMPETENCE.

• • • • • •

The Invention of Happiness

Some may argue that happiness is life itself. I would bet my house on the fact that when you held your newborn in your arms and gazed lovingly into their eyes, your biggest wish wasn't that they learn algebra or that they would one day be able to grapple with Newtonian physics. As they looked adoringly up at you, sucking on their fist, you didn't wish that they learned a couple of Shakespeare plays or got to grade 3 clarinet. Nope, you had (and still have) just one wish for your children – that they're happy. Indeed, in a global survey, happiness easily topped the list of what people want for their children and grandchildren.

But why?

Well, partly because you intuitively know what the science of positive psychology keeps telling us – happiness is good for you. On a small scale, happier people catch fewer colds and on a massive scale, they live longer. One of my favourite studies is David Snowdon's oft-quoted study of nuns in which he analysed diary entries and found that nuns whose diaries were full of happiness, joy and hope lived as much as ten years longer than your average nun.[32]

Evidence suggests that the happiness/health causation runs both ways, so health is one of the strongest predictors of happiness, especially in the old. Frequent smiling is reported to have many therapeutic and health benefits particularly when the smile is a 'Duchenne' – a heartfelt passionate beam that lights up your face. This is why you want it for your children. But here's the real clincher: your happiness is bigger than you – it also benefits those around you. When you feel great you are enhancing the lives of family, friends, work colleagues and customers.

Even amidst a chapter that has God as a central theme, I don't want to sound overly evangelical, but I'm not far off in suggesting that the pursuit and eventual experiencing of happiness could be described as your moral duty. Happiness (in line with all other emotions) is an evolutionary adaptation that exists to make us engage in certain behaviours that will optimize our chances of surviving and reproducing. There's an argument that says happiness is a relatively modern emotional add-on. Happiness is absent from Steven Pinker's four hard-wired emotional programmes (cleverly labelled as 'the 4 Fs': feeding, fighting, fleeing and sexual behaviour).[33] These primitive impulses are basically about the survival of yourself or the species. But no 'happiness'? The inference is that cavemen didn't waste time thinking about whether they were happy or not, or whether their life had meaning. They were too busy surviving. It's just about possible that we invented 'happiness' when survival became more certain. It was only then that a new layer of brain was bolted on, right at the front. This neo-cortex serves useful purposes beyond merely allowing you to wear a hat. We were already aligned with just about every other species, in that our emotions are an open loop – they transfer to others. If you watch the bunny rabbits munching on lush meadow grass, it only takes one to be spooked before there's a rush of white tails bobbing into the hedgerows. It's a matter of survival.

All emotions are valid. They all serve a purpose. Happiness is a particularly interesting emotional adaptation. It switches your brain on, fostering creativity and visions of a wonderful future. Our bigger brains also give us a vast emotional spectrum. I doubt that lower order creatures feel the same range of emotions. Does a limpet feel joy? Or, shimmying up the ladder of sophistication, does an anteater get emotional on a rainy Monday?

I'd suggest that there are two vastly undervalued emotions: optimism and hope. Indeed, without them, our ancestors might never have ventured far from their tribes and we might all be cave dwellers, still huddled together and dreaming of light and heat. Emotions work in a loop with your thinking. Crucial in all of this is that your current mood affects your thinking in three important ways.

Firstly, when you're in a chipper mood, you think fast and effortlessly. You are more creative and willing to take a bit of a risk so optimism means you have a tendency to give things a go. The opposite is true when you are in a negative mood. You can become fixated on the problem, ruminating and worrying so hard that a solution is hard to come by. Thinking is slow, ponderous and circuitous. Your default answer is a sure-fire 'can't do'.

Secondly, mood also affects what you remember. If you're in a good mood and someone asks you about life you're more likely to colour things positively and, once again, the opposite is true if you're in a bad mood.

But thirdly, and potentially most profoundly, your present mood affects your decision making and therefore your future. Moods can be hot or cold. So when you're feeling the heat of hunger, you buy more food than you need because you imagine your hunger will last forever. Upbeat moods mean that your future looks bright and your ambitious goals seem achievable, so you are spurred on to do your best to get there. On a more disturbing level of 'hot' moods, Berkeley students exposed to pornography reported much higher preparedness to engage in more 'exotic' sexual encounters. They rated as 25 per cent less likely to use a condom and, bizarrely, sexual contact with animals was 72 per cent more likely. So 'hot emotions' don't necessarily lead to good choices. *Baaaaa!*

And when you're in a negative or 'cold' state, you view the future through your current bleakness and nothing looks worthwhile. *I'll never get a girlfriend so there's no point even going out and trying* becomes a self-fulfilling prophecy. Your pessimism means those huge goals are just pie in the sky.

You slump into the torpor of *I'm never going to get any sex, not even with a goat.* Your thoughts are a burden.

But all of this assumes a very big question, one that goes to the heart of theology and anthropology and stems from the mere thought of having sex with animals: 'have we evolved at all?'

Harold, Daisy, Abdul, Raj and the Blobfish

This is how it is. We don't know your starting point so to absolve us of any offence, we're going to introduce you to 'Harold' and 'Daisy', not their real names. Harold has been brought up to believe the world was created by a divine being who spent six days moulding the earth, potter's wheel style, designing all the creatures and then having a breather on day seven. In an act of supreme sacrifice, the divine being sent his son down to teach us a few lessons, most notably on how we should live our lives. 'Humbly' is the one-word answer. A slightly longer list got immortalized in ten golden rules carved on a rock. Harold's not sure where that stone is but he knows that if everybody abided by the top ten, the world would be a fab place.

Harold knows this because it says so in an ancient book. He does sometimes wonder why it was all set in the Middle East and why they all had English sounding names. Sure, 'Jesus' sounds a bit foreign, but Peter, Simon and Andrew? Really? But Harold's not meant to question the book, merely accept it as a truth that's been passed down through the generations. After all, the book has been around since the birth of the planet, an amazing 2000 or so years ago. It frustrates Harold that his work colleague Abdul has a different book, with similar characters and similar stories. Abdul swears that his book is true. As for Harold's next door neighbour, well, he's just bonkers. Raj also has a book and his book has hundreds of Gods – some even have elephant heads. I mean, how can Raj believe what is essentially a picture book? But he does.

And then there's Daisy, a thoroughly modern gal who believes the universe was created in a big bang of something or other, and that we're perched, somewhat precariously, on a ball of rock that is hurtling through space in a Goldilocks orbit that happens to sustain life. It was a trillion to one chance that life sparked at all but over millions of years, evolution has whittled out the weaklings and ironed our imperfections to create human beings as they are today. Daisy believes that other species have also been busy evolving, hence anteaters have long noses and snails have eyes on stalks. Daisy's theory also explains fossils and why we keep digging up burial sites in which our ancestors had smaller heads. Survival of the fittest means that we've gradually evolved and are continuing to do so. She does sometimes wonder why monkeys have stopped evolving and she once Googled 'blobfish' and wondered why they exist at all?

Rather discombobulatingly, our starting point is that both Harold and Daisy are right. And so are Abdul and Raj. A 'belief' is something ingrained in your head and, to you, it's true. So who are we to argue?

In terms of happiness, it matters quite a lot. If we take the blobfish example, Harold believes it was created and put on earth by God. It is a divine creature, beautifully designed, with a purpose.

Daisy wonders whether lying on the sea bed waiting for food to float into your mouth might be a bit of a waste of time. She's particularly concerned that you don't Google 'picture of blobfish' for fear that you won't sleep tonight.

Daisy's lack of belief in God means that nobody's coming to save her. Nobody is going to mark Daisy out for greatness. Fairy godmothers don't exist and, as for a real God swashbuckling away on her behalf, it's a nice thought. Daisy imagines that, after all this time, there might be some proper evidence? She knows that Harold will point to 'him up there' sending his son to die on the cross as 'evidence'. Really? she wonders. Was Harold there? Is Harold's ancient book true? Christians, Sikhs, Jews, Muslims, Jehovah, Jedis (and the rest) have books that they absolutely swear by, and each religion has factions that say their bit is right. Daisy knows that all those books are different but if you ask the followers, each is totally convinced that theirs is true. So convinced they're willing to go to war over it. Are they all right? Or none of them? Daisy has no idea but rather than waiting for God to choose her, she's decided to pick herself. Daisy has decided to quit waiting and make something magical happen. She's putting effort into living an inspiring worldly life. Daisy has decided to be her own big break.

Harold is a bit more relaxed. His belief is that whoever created the earth is still there, looking over us. Perhaps even watching out for us? After all, if 'He' created us, then it stands to reason that He has a vested interest in our ongoing health and wellbeing. Harold reckons he's onto a long-term sure-fire winner. Dangling in the distance is a big orange eternal carrot. All Harold has to do is behave reasonably and abide by the ten golden rules, and there's an eternal afterlife with his name on it. Plus, there's a safety net! If Harold does have a bad day, he can confess and his sins are forgiven, like a big morality reset button.

For Harold, no matter whether life is good or bad, there's a better one waiting in the wings. The religions seem to have one thing in common – they are all promising that, if you believe in their creed, you will be guaranteed an afterlife party of epic proportions. It's a cool way of asking you to put up with a pretty mundane worldly existence because if you can just get by in this one, there's a much better eternal one. All you have to do to access your free pass to eternal glory, is to behave reasonably well. Oh, and die.

The difference between those who have a religious belief and those who don't is the safety net. Life is a perilous tight-rope walk for all but, for non-believers, the advice is don't look down!

> **Comforting thought in a box**
>
> *I don't sit around pondering the prospect of death. However, seeing as it's inevitable for myself and everyone I know, it's worth considering the final moments.*
>
> *Picture the scene, in which you're holding the hand of a loved one. The end is nigh. Your loved one looks up at you and asks, 'Where am I going?'*
>
> *You don't know. Nobody really knows, although there are a fair few who will claim they do. So how about this – have you ever considered where you were before you were conceived? Because that's probably where you're going back to.*

Cloud 9

Let's dare to broaden the view. Engage your wildest imagination and go with the flow ...

Grab a bunch of helium balloons and, like the old chap in the movie *Up!*, float up into the sky. Perch yourself on a cloud, legs a-swinging, and have a good look at the world below. You'll notice a lot of people scurrying around. And there you are. Crikey, you're in a rush too.

What you'll soon notice from up here is that you are playing a part in life and you're interacting with other characters, but you're not the director of the show. You're a tiny dot of energy, buzzing around. In physics, the energy of life would be referred to as the quantum field. In religion it'd be God. Either way, it's something beyond me and thee.

Everything is energy. It's mostly invisible, yes, but it's everywhere. In the next chapter we're going to link thought with energy and argue that without thought there would be no experience and no perception. Indeed, thought is the creator of your world. But for now, just watch everyone scurrying down there and maybe dare to ask yourself, why are they scurrying?

For centuries, human beings scurried and toiled in the hope that the afterlife would be their sanctuary. Nowadays, we'll take the bold argument that religion (Christian-based), at least in this country, is slipping away. We might also argue that in other countries, the religious tide is still coming in. But, right here, right now, as science sweeps in and religion recedes, it exposes a vast expanse of nothingness, like Morecambe Bay at low tide.

Blob Theory

Did someone say 'Morecambe'? That's where our illustrious co-author Andy W was born and brought up. So this must be his bit? We love him for lots of reasons, most notably the fact that he was disappointed to find this so-called 'English breakfast tea' doesn't have any sausage or bacon in it.

Andy C makes writing look easy. For me, it's a process that involves sitting staring at a blank sheet of paper until the drops of blood form on my forehead. So, where do I start? How about a subject I failed at school, physics?

I think the Newtonian law, 'energy can be neither created nor destroyed' remains one of the hard and fast rules of science. I've lost track of what's what since Higgs boson and the Hadron Collider suggested that atoms can be in several places at once. And I have to put aside the fact that some of the meetings I've sat through have certainly robbed me of every atom of energy.

Those issues aside, I have recently postulated something that I'm calling 'blob theory'. I'm thinking that if it's to go mainstream it might need a better name? But when I explained it to the other Andy, he told me it already has another name. In fact, apparently it's the basis for several very well-known religions.

Blob theory is in line with Newton's 'energy can be neither created nor destroyed' punchy one-liner. We are existing in a hermetically sealed breathable atmosphere where energy sloshes around. It changes form (the sun shines, flowers grow, bees make honey which I enjoy on toast and it gives me energy ...) but we can't create any more of it, or indeed, get rid of any. There's a fixed amount of energy buzzing around in our atmospheric bubble.

You and I are part of that energy system. Admittedly, we're tiny specs rather than major players, but we act as pinpricks of life in the enormity of 'the blob'. We're born, we live, we die. When we pass away, our energy becomes subsumed back into the 'big blobness', with the inevitability that we (our energy) has to pop up somewhere else.

Some religions might choose to interpret this literally, so you come back, for example, as a wombat. Or you might experience rebirth as another person, coming back time after time, in different incarnations. Some strands of karmic thinking suggest you keep coming back until you've learned a lesson.

On a non-literal level, your tiny pinprick of energy is recycled, probably not as a discrete thing or person, but you certainly reappear in the system somewhere. In fact, you cannot NOT reappear. You are energy and, as such, are subject to Newtonian Law – you can be neither created nor destroyed. Blob Theory™ (yes, I've this minute decided to trade mark it) says you've been around pretty much forever and, good news, you will continue to exist forever (albeit maybe someday as a blobfish – remember don't Google it!)

There exists the vexed issue of the soul and your consciousness. What are they and where the heck do they go? Seed planted, we'll grapple with them in the 'Land of Knowing'. For now, rejoice in the comforting thought that whether you believe in God or not, you will indeed be around for all eternity.

But so will Donald Trump.

Guns or Roses?

So, having skirted around it, we're back to the question, does God make you happier?

There's plenty of research that suggests so. However, it's less likely to be one's belief in God or the act of praying that nudges the happy-ometer needle above average. It's more the socializing and relationships formed as part of a congregation. We already know that God works in mysterious ways and now it seems he also works in happiness subterfuge. 'Belief' means we feel compelled to build churches, temples, mosques and synagogues bringing like-minded folk together in worship and friendship. Ironically, the result is a big bang of happiness.

As for my research? Strap yourself in because it's a teeny bit controversial – the end-game of my thesis was to uncover the so-called 'intentional strategies' used by happy people. And, guess what, with regard to 'religious faith makes me happy' I found a significant statistical difference between happy and less happy people... so far so good... but that it was the less happy people who answered in the affirmative. Stated in the opposite way, happy people are less likely to rate religion as a reason for their happiness. For reasons of me being out of my depth, I chose not to major on this in the write-up and, to be fair, it does go against many findings from other researchers.

Our aim is not to persuade you either way on the God question (largely because we don't actually know). If you're a devout believer in anything, this book isn't going to change your mind. Maybe the happiness learning is this ... for the believers, of whatever religion, to stop putting all your eggs in the heavenly basket. You can't be 100 per cent certain so while we sincerely hope the afterlife will be amazing, you may as well take the opportunity to live it up while you're in your worldly form. Terrifyingly, you might come back as a blobfish? So turn your happiness dial up a notch or two and let it all hang out. Not ridiculously so, but why not be a living breathing example of happiness. Shine baby, shine.

For the non-believers? Ditto! You can't be 100 per cent certain either! You might end up knock-knock-knocking on heaven's door, so you may as well be awesomely happy while also doing your darnedest to live by the ten-tabled rules. Thus, the same advice applies; you are infinite energy so shine baby, shine.

The Ten Tweetable #happinesscommandments

The original ten commandments are getting on a bit. Plus, they're written negatively, couched in 'Thou shall not...' language. So we're suggesting a modern rewrite in positive language. Here are our Ten Commandments of Happiness, couched in 'Thou shall...' terms.

1. Thou shall make an effort to be as upbeat as the situation allows.
2. Thou shall talk to as many people as possible. Yes, even strangers!
3. Thou shall find time for face-to-face relationships and cut down on social media.
4. Thou shall appreciate many more moments.
5. Thou shall be grateful to have functioning kidneys, beating heart, etc.
6. Thou shall increase thou's smiling by 40 per cent, thus infecting other people with thou's happiness,
7. Thou shall work out what thou's strengths are and play to them.
8. Thou shall quit low-level grumbling about first-world problems.
9. Thou shall catch others doing things well and tell them.
10. Thou shall take personal responsibility for being thou's best self.

Feel free to tweet any you think we might have missed?

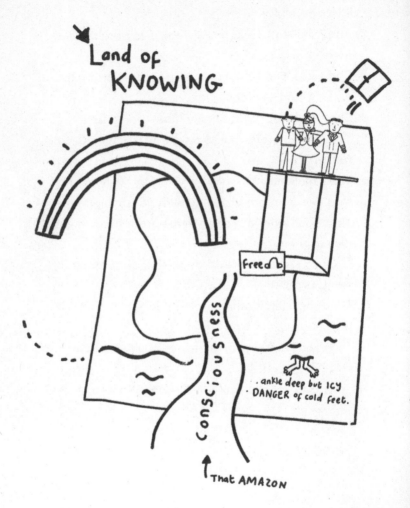

Chapter 8
THE OASIS OF KNOWING

• • • • • •

In which we move to a land way beyond clever, where even this introduction is like, wowza!

Can you hear that faint wailing? If you get your binocs, you'll see the academics left behind on Boffin Island. There they are, lining the shore, jumping up and down, pulling their hair out and jabbing their fingers in our direction. I can't make out their exact words but, from the looks on their faces, it's probably a good job! As you can see, it's not far from Boffin Island and the sea is only ankle deep, but these boffins are prone to getting very cold feet.

The Oasis of Knowing immigration police don't check your passports, they check your CV. Anyone can come in, but qualifications can be a burden. Please note the name of this particular land – it's less about 'proving' and more about 'knowing'.

No big intro needed. There are just two things in this oasis, but they're MASSIVE – the Amazon and a great glass elevator.

It helps if you put your brain into neutral. Earmuffs on so you can't hear the screaming academics, and off we go …

••••••

SOBREMESA (SPANISH): WHEN THE FOOD IS GONE BUT THE CONVERSATION IS STILL FLOWING.

••••••

www.amazonswim.com

'Agnotology' is the study of ignorance. More generally, the term also highlights the increasingly common condition where increased knowledge of a subject leaves one more uncertain than before.

On first reading of this chapter you might temporarily experience acute agnotologism, a paradoxical *it makes perfect sense but no sense whatsoever?* kind of feeling. If this happens we suggest you read this chapter again. And maybe again after that. If, after a third time it still makes 'perfect but absolutely no sense', you're too clever.

There's a reason why most personal development doesn't include this material. Here's our best shot ...

I watched a programme about a bonkers guy who decided to swim the Amazon (for younger readers, the Amazon is a very long river named after an online book shop). Let me point out the obvious, not only is it a stupidly long river, but it has crocs and piranhas. Oh, and I almost forgot to say, he swam *upstream*, against the current.

So, he got himself wet-suited, goggled, rubbed down with croc repellent and in he went. The mouth of the Amazon is a huge delta of vast brownness. Our hero lasted less than an hour before he was hit by a floating VW campervan and had to seek medical attention. It wasn't long before he was back in, front-crawling his way uphill. Mile after painful mile his arms turned and legs kicked. He encountered all sorts of hazards, including the aforementioned crocs and bitey fish.

We will leave him front-crawling against the current and return later to see how he got on.

The Elevator of Awareness

Most people don't buy personal development books. There-fore, you are not 'most people'. Those who buy them don't always read them. I've been to households where they have a Deepak Chopra (the book, not the bloke) lying around on the coffee table, an unthumbed nod to what they think might be cool.

You've got to The Oasis of Knowing so we want to reward you with a chapter that adds stretch marks to your thinking. It would be too ego-inflated to suggest it's the best personal development chapter that's ever been written, so we won't. Instead, we'll default to my literary hero, Roald Dahl, who had tremendous fun writing about a great glass elevator, so we thought we'd try it out too.

Having visited all of the previous lands, you are already pretty high up. Higher than most. From up here you can see that you may not be the person you want to be, but at least you have the self-awareness to notice what you're unhappy with and the desire to do something about it. You are part of the first generation in human history that has truly discovered we are always capable of improving our lives – socially, emotionally, professionally and financially. So, these dratted infernally well-hidden 'secrets' of happiness; where to start looking? Well, pretty much from sentence one, we've warned you that it's as much about knowing how to look, as it is where to look.

You have figured that the 'where' bit is easy. You can basically stop the search. If you're in hot pursuit of happiness then simply kick your Nike's off and stop running. Happiness is here.

Real insight comes from a higher level of consciousness that dares to examine *how* to look.

That's a weird sentence. What does it even mean?

Back into the great glass elevator. Let's ascend one more level ...

Copycats

Stanley Milgram's famous sidewalk experiments are core syllabus material for every psychology student in the world.[34] He positioned a 'stimulus crowd' in the street, ranging in number from 1 to 15 people and, on cue, these people would stand and look up at a window on the sixth floor for precisely one minute. There was nothing there. They'd just stare, with Stan filming the results. What fabulous fun.

He found that 4 per cent joined in with a single starer and 40 per cent joined in with 15 starers. So copying behaviour is influenced by the size of the crowd. The point is that you can't help doing what other people do. The modern example is a motorway accident. You curse the rubberneckers as you wait for your turn to gawp at the police sweeping someone up.

So, we are conditioned to copy behaviours. Ditto emotions. The self-help literature has lurched towards 'Nobody can make you feel anything. You are in charge of your feelings'. Technically, at its purest level, this is true. But it's eye-wateringly impractical. We have evolved to understand feelings, both our own and other people's. Empathy is a crucial driver of human evolution and it would be to our detriment if we stopped connecting.

It's true that emotion creates motion – so how we feel drives our behaviour. The trick is to generate brilliant feelings, ones that give you energy and serve you well. But how? If we're programmed to copy everyone else, and they're stuck in 'minor glumness', aren't we doomed to feel the same?

No. If you follow emotions upstream you'll arrive at their source – thinking. Emotions are nothing more than a mental construct that starts in your head.

Let's start simply ...

One morning a little girl tugs on her mother's apron and asks, 'Mummy, what's positive psychology?' (like you would!) Her mum smiles sweetly down at her adorable daughter and says, 'You see Grandpa over there, why don't you go and ask him about his arthritis. And when he tells you, make sure he shares all his aches and pains.'

So the little girl trots through the kitchen to the old fella who is sitting watching TV and pipes up, 'Grandpa, can you tell me about Arthur-itis? And,' she adds wagging a finger, 'don't you go missing out any of your aches and pains.'

Her grandpa slumps deep into his chair and takes a big sigh as he considers all his aches and pains. He puffs out his cheeks and glances at his granddaughter. 'Well,' he says, 'the first thing you need to know is that I wouldn't wish arthritis on my worst enemy. My joints have swelled so everywhere aches you see. Toes,' he says pointing a crooked finger towards his feet. 'Knees. Hips. My wrists are swollen and looky here,' he says, holding out his hands. The little girl peers closely at his crooked fingers, the joints swollen with old age. 'I can't even grip a cup of tea anymore,' he says. 'Old man's hands! Where've they come from?'

Her grandpa takes another lungful of oxygen and uses it to sigh a very big sigh. 'Know what?' he says, 'I lay in bed this morning, listening to the rain on the window, feeling the pain in my joints and I thought, "What's the point? Why even bother getting out of bed?"'

The little girl had got her information. 'Thanks for that grandpa,' she says, skipping back to the kitchen. 'Mummy,' she says, 'Grandpa says his Arthur-itis is very painful. He's got bad toes and bad knees and old man's hands that he doesn't know where they've come from. So now will you tell me what positive psychology is?'

Her mum adopts that smug smile of knowingness, as though she were featuring in a story from a self-help book and says, 'Well done little lady. Now go and ask your grandpa about the best holiday he's ever had.'

The daughter skips off, back to the old chap, with a singy, 'Grandpa, tell me about the best holiday you've ever had.'

A broad grin lights up the old man's face. He leans forward and his granddaughter sees a rare sparkle in his eye. He rubs his arthritic hands together as he ponders aloud. 'We've had dozens of fabulous holidays little lady,' he muses, 'but if I had to choose the very best one, I'd say it was in Great Yarmouth in 1963, because that's where I met your grandma ...' And the old boy goes on to tell the fantastic story of his holiday in 1963.

It's a beautiful story that's not trying to be funny or complicated, but is a fabulous way of capturing the essence of inside-out thinking. Let's take a quick peek at the learning.

First of all, grandpa's demeanour has changed. His new thoughts have flooded him with happy chemicals and he's sitting bolt upright rubbing his arthritic hands in glee. Is the old man cured? Of course not, but he has shifted his focus away from the burdens of his condition to something brighter and this has had a near-miraculous effect.

Secondly, how quickly has this happened? Answer – in an instant!

Thirdly, and crucially, how has it happened? How has the arthritic old man been transformed into a sparkly-eyed wonder-filled cauldron of exuberance? We can go around the houses with this one but it boils down to asking a better question. The second question changed the old man's thoughts, eliciting a whole gush of positive emotions that resulted in a bout of instant aliveness.

And that immediately got me thinking: how often do I talk to people and get the worst out of them because of how I talk to them? On a literal level, how can I change the way I talk to my own granddad? And, on a bigger penny-dropping level, what if the change of thinking needs to start with me?

Gulp!

So I changed. Over the last few years I've come to the conclusion that it's not what we don't know that keeps us from growing and learning, it's more the case that we think we know and we close our minds to what's possible.

Back into the elevator. Up we go again, to the next level of possibility...

Riveting

......

'WE HAVE THE MOST WONDERFUL JOB IN THE WORLD. WE FIND PEOPLE IN VARIOUS STAGES OF SLEEP. AND THEN WE GET TO TAP THEM ON THE SHOULDER AND BE WITH THEM AS THEY WAKE UP TO THE MAGNIFICENCE OF LIFE.'

......

Sydney Banks

People get epiphanies – bolt-from-the-blue moments of pure enlightenment that can happen to pretty much anyone at any time. Archimedes had his in the bath but mostly, I would imagine, they happen in and around church.

Here's an epiphany that happened in the shipyards of Glasgow. Syd Banks was, by all accounts, as ordinary as you can get until one day, while working as part of a team constructing a warship in the Clyde shipyards, he had an epiphany that everything is about thought. *Whoosh!* Syd's realization was that humankind has been living a big fat lie. Your whole world isn't happening to you, it's constructed by you, via thought and consciousness.

As far as we know, Syd hadn't read books on philosophy, he knew nothing about the law of attraction, Buddhism or mindfulness – he was just cracking on at work and suddenly, out of the blue, a realization that changed his life. Syd's notion is both simple and incredibly complex at the same time.

The simplicity lies in the fact not that you have thoughts that create your world, but that you are the thinker. I promise you, that is a very big thought. You could describe Syd's day at work as 'riveting', in all senses of the word.

So, your thoughts create your world. What's more, some of your thoughts aren't even yours, they're hand-me-downs that have become accepted truths. You've learned them from the media or your parents. I was told I was shocking at maths (age 11) and, guess what, I'm shocking at maths now.

Most people are too busy to rethink the way they think – or even to spend much time thinking at all. Syd suggests you feel your thinking. So, hang onto your hat lest it falls off when you raise your eyebrows in wonder; it becomes less about controlling thought and more about the simple realization that you are the thinker.

Before we go any further, let's pause for a very quick example. Have you ever read an email and got angry? Inside-out thinking says the pixels on the screen have made you angry. They are a jumble of images that you have learned to form into words, to which you've attached a meaning, which has created a thought of 'unfairness', to which you associate an emotion of 'indignation' – and off you go, jabbing away at a curt reply.

It links with Garret Kramer's concept of 'stillpower', the opposite of 'willpower', which is an understanding that self-worth has nothing to do with external events like winning, parental approval, fame, having a big yacht or, indeed, terse emails.[35] It is simply that our state of mind determines our view of the outside world.

So thinking is a forgery and life situations are neutral. Are they really? This is a toughie. The idea of rational thought dampening down our road rage is a nice theory but chasing them across town can be more satisfying. Justifying to yourself why your inferior colleague got promoted ahead of you is great in your head. But letting their tyres down is what you actually do.

> Thought for the day
>
> *Worry is (very often but not always) like walking through a haunted house. It's an illusion.*

Still with me? Good. Then, back into the elevator.

Brace yourself, here's the next level of agnotology. Lift doors closing, we're going waaaay up...

The Dark Room

••••••

'THE FOOL ONLY KNOWS WHAT HE THINKS; THE WISE MAN KNOWS HE'S THE THINKER.'

••••••

Syd Banks

Check the view from up here! The higher the lift ascends, the weirder the views. This one is pretty much anything you want it to be. There's a physical you, but there's another you, experiencing the physical you. Think of it like this, the flesh and blood you allows your consciousness to get around town. The 'you' you see in the mirror is just a means of transport.

While you're wandering around town, what does your brain see? The rather disturbing answer is 'absolutely nothing'. How can it 'see'? Your brain is locked away in a dark and silent chamber, called a skull. Not only can it not see, it also cannot hear, touch, smell or taste.

Your senses detect stimuli 'out there' and translate them into a language that the brain can understand. So sight, hearing, touch, smell and taste aren't real – as David Eagleman so eloquently describes, 'they are an electrochemical rendition in a dark theatre'.[36]

Let's take an example of you walking on a beach, breathing in the salty sea air. First up, and rather disturbingly, the

139

sand's yellow colour doesn't really exist. It's no colour at all, until some electromagnetic radiation hits your retina and is converted into something your brain (in its sealed container) computes as 'yellow'. And the waves have no sound. Yes, the waves are there. They are a 'thing', emitting electromagnetic radiation and soundwaves, but it's only inside your head that this becomes a crashing ocean.

And as for smelling that sea air, that's just another creation. Reality is odourless; there's no such thing as 'smell' outside our brains. 'Smell' is a mass of molecules floating about in the air that your nose receptors process and turn into what we call a 'smell'. Our brain then matches it against a database of previous experiences and comes up with 'salty sea air' and, whoosh, we've made sense of the moment.

We believe our experience of the walk to be real, but it's entirely constructed from inside the sealed container. Hence, reality isn't, in fact, anything of the sort.

We understand if this is as high as you want the lift to take you. It's a lot further than most people ever get. But there is one more level – 'rooftop' – from which you can see everything. We dare you! Come on, let's go to the very top floor...

Roof with a View

> *Baby eagles learn to fly by being pushed out of the nest. They have 500 feet to learn!*

Check out the view from here. It's totally magnificent, yet completely unreal. There's one more vital ingredient in the illusion. Your 'reality' is determined by how you allocate your attention and this one thing – attention – is the glue that holds your life together. There are so many stimuli vying for your attention that your brain has to narrow them down, hence what you focus on becomes your reality.

And so, looking out on the view from up here, we begin to glimpse consciousness. The easy and yet supremely complex answer to 'who's doing your thinking?' is, of course, you. So who the heck are you? *You* are a powder keg of liquid and chemicals, surrounded by skin, but all the *I* stuff is intangible. Your sense of 'self' comes from a whole mishmash of experiences, beliefs, roles, thoughts, ideas, feelings and cultural ties.

The overwhelming idea is that your self-image is a belief. Oh my gosh, even that's not real! You are real enough but the idea of who you are has been formed over your lifetime. The image you have of you has become imprinted on your subconscious and it's taken on a life of its own. You have become your own self-image. That's why confident people act confidently and negative people spot negativity.

Your consciousness allows you to create a script, the internal dialogue that becomes the narrative of your life. Syd Banks is bang in line with the other wonder of modern philosophy, Richard Wilkins, in suggesting that your sense of who you are has been so well practised that you've forgotten it's just words.[37] Indeed, you can't get rid of the script because you wrote it!

Banks' and Wilkins' knee-shaker is that you can't escape from the script, all you can do is realize it's a script and step outside of it. Applying it to the classic road rage scenario one last time (I'm using this because it's familiar to most people), you experience some discourteous driving and your script tells you you've been violated in some way. It may only be a small thing but you've learned that you're supposed to get angry and before you know it, your heart is racing and so are you, chasing the other driver across town.

Recognizing that it is merely a script allows you to step outside of it and make a better choice, hence a calmer approach to this particular situation. Indeed, a simple question such as 'How would the very best version of me respond to this situation?' is a decent starting point.

... Which takes us back to our hero, front-crawling against the flow of the mighty Amazon. As he progressed, the river gradually narrowed and, miraculously, it also got cleaner. Several weeks in and he was swimming through crystal clear water, cutting a swathe through the magnificent rainforest.

In a bit of an anticlimax he failed to find the source of the Amazon. Indeed, there are many sources, all of which are crystal clear springs. No crocs, no piranhas and no VW camper vans. Syd's inside-out thinking says that all of us have access to the clear and un-muddied source of our thoughts, but we end up latching onto the wrong ones. Often these thoughts can be bitey or stingy and once in a while a VW camper van of negative thought will do us some serious damage.

You can learn this stuff at an intellectual level and try practising it as a technique and it won't work. You end up over-analysing. Indeed, 'analysing' can get in the way of 'knowing'. That's why the academics are screaming so loudly. 'Prove it, damn you. Give us some evidence!'

I don't think you need any more evidence than the latest ONS data that shows there were 58 million anti-depressant prescriptions written in England last year.[38] Our thoughts are killing us! And if you dare to fight against them, the effort of trying to remain upbeat can wear you out. 'Positive thinking' means you have to take your current negative thought and give it a spin. It's an ongoing wrestling match – you against you – and you end up beating yourself to a pulp. Back to the PhD. What if my flourishing people have achieved a breakthrough without really knowing? They just intuitively do this stuff. It's beyond 'clever' (as measured by qualifications).

First of all, it's about being aware that you have a choice of thoughts and, secondly, that you focus your attention on the good ones. The essence is that thoughts are streaming by and whichever you choose to focus on becomes your reality. So, at one level, it makes good sense to wait for a good one. But applying some effort to generating some nice thoughts and learning to give them a positive spin surely means that your river of consciousness will contain many more resourceful thoughts.

In the Amazon analogy, inside-out thinking is about sourcing purity of thought. If you were able to access a higher level of consciousness and realize that everything was created from thought, you wouldn't have to fish the crocs, piranhas and VWs out – they simply wouldn't be in there because, guess what, it's you who put them in there in the first place.

Top Tips

Three new ways of thinking with regards to your script:

1. Think of a situation in which you struggle. For example, doing a presentation to your senior management team. Your script is telling you that you're not very comfortable with this. Imagine you've borrowed someone else's script. In fact, you're reading from the script of 'the most confident presenter in the world'. Have a go at doing what their script says.

2. Your script is only written up to this point. Have a leaf through it. What lessons has it taught you that you can apply going forward?

3. Things always look brighter when you're on holiday so our advice is to take a mental vacation. But only one of 'you' can go. Send the old cranky version of you to Tahiti for a couple of weeks. While you're away, inhabit the new super-positive, glow-on-the-outside you, even when you're on your own. Source some fabulous thoughts. Read from the 'new you' script for two weeks and see how you get on. If it doesn't work out, you can always welcome the cranky you back after a fortnight? Guaranteed, it will have had a rubbish time in paradise.

Chapter 9

THE FOREST OF NEGATIVITY

• • • • • •

In which we navigate through a forest blacked out by negativity.

Here we talk about the dreaded 'black dog' of depression, making the point that this chapter is more about the grey spaniel of glumness. And, sticking with dogs, we already know that owners look like their dogs but did you know that, over a lifetime, partners end up looking like each other? Sit tight, all will be revealed.

We tiptoe through mediocrity, being careful to avoid the Pollyanna school of unbridled optimism, and stride out purposefully onto the vast plains of bad news. We explain how and why you're programmed for negativity before diving into the choppy waters of 'provocative therapy' and rescuing ourselves with a wonderful bedtime story.

We offer a couple of adages and, after a bit of rain-bathing, we grab a shovel and start digging into your past where we find a whole load of terrifying skeletons dancing in the darkness. Thankfully, we apply some 'ordinary magic' and they can finally rest in peace.

Phew!

Welcome to The Forest of Negativity where the branches are so dense that they block out the sunlight. If you look up, you can see it, peeping through? Just occasionally that is. But most people are looking down. There are lots of paths into the forest, but only one out. You might see a lot of people just wandering, aimlessly, like lost souls. Many people have been here so long they call it home.

Please stick close to your tour guide and look out for the woman who wasn't for risk taking and a budgerigar who most definitely was.

Heads down, off we go …

••••••

JUGAAD (HINDI): THE ABILITY TO GET BY.

••••••

Worried to Death

Think of this chapter as a Burlesque dancer, gradually peel-ing away some of the layers until there's nothing left to hide behind. Nothing, that is, except your thoughts.

So let's start with a reminder of just how powerful they are ...

Nick Sitzman was a fit, healthy and strong young man who worked as part of a train crew. By all accounts Nick was a great guy with one major fault, he was a worrier. His fam-ily describe him as someone who worried about everything and always feared the worst. One midsummer day, the foreman announced that it was his birthday so the train crew were dismissed an hour early. Nick was accidentally locked in a refrigerator boxcar, and the rest of the workmen left the site. Nick panicked, banging and shouting until his fists were bloody and his voice was hoarse. No one heard him. Wanting to let his wife and family know exactly what had happened to him, Nick found a knife and began to etch words on the wooden floor. He wrote, 'It's so cold, my body is getting numb. If I could just go to sleep. These may be my last words.'

The next morning the crew slid open the heavy doors of the boxcar and found Nick dead. An autopsy revealed that every physical sign of his body indicated he had frozen to death. And yet the refrigeration unit of the car was inoperative.

Nick had literally worried himself to death.

Nick's story is an urban myth, an exaggeration of the truth that your thoughts can damage your health. We're not suggesting that it's never appropriate to stress, complain or get upset, more that some people spend an exorbitant chunk of time engaged in negative thinking without realizing it. It's easy to become a well-practised finely tuned neg-head, with an accumulated lifetime of tutting.

Anything you want, you have to create, and that includes your world, starting inside-out. Neuroplasticity is one of those rare six-syllabled words that is actually quite easy to fathom. Your brain is malleable. The firing and wiring of neurons gives us hope that real change and personal growth can actually happen, whatever age we are.

Everyone is able to change. The bigger question is, are you willing? It's easy to get stuck in a neurological rut – and become what I call 'hard of thinking'. I did a talk at the Women's Institute – 30 ladies, and I hate to stereotype but they were mostly of a certain age. They were lovely people and my semi-humorous talk was warmly received by all except Gladys (I've changed her name to protect her. Her actual name was Joan). I've never had an octogenarian heckler before so I let her go on until the other ladies got embarrassed and shushed her up.

Gladys, it transpired, was miserable and, by all accounts, always had been. She sat, arms folded, lips straight, and pretty much personified Thatcher's catchphrase of 'this lady's not for turning'. I sometimes get drawn into heated debates with teenagers who sit steadfastly unsmiling and rooted to misery but Gladys was 82. She perhaps knows better than me?

My message is that, whatever your age, you can wake up from living on autopilot. If we practise new ways of responding, the old connections become weaker and new connections grow. Gladys, on reflection, is a great example of someone for whom that just isn't going to work because to stand a glimmer, you have to open up your mind to the possibility.

I failed to even get a foot in the door of Gladys' mind. I don't think she even put the chain on and opened the door a crack.

Please don't mistake this passage as being about Gladys (or Joan). When insight comes knocking, at least open the door and listen with an open mind. That way you create some choices – you can let insight in or choose to slam the door in its face. I use Gladys as a lesson to myself: stay open-minded. And if someone offers to give up his evening and do a talk, for free, even if it's a really bad talk, smile and be nice.

Happy (but not too clappy)

There's a massive difference between 'clinical depression' and 'minor glumness' – this chapter is about the latter. Depression is an horrific experience that can be brought about by chemical imbalances and/or loneliness and/or dreadful times. There's the oft-quoted statistic that one in four of us will suffer at some point. There are various remedies of which 'snapping out of it' isn't one.

Minor glumness, on the other hand, is completely snappable out of. It's nothing to do with chemical imbalances and much more to do with sinking into bad (dare I even venture to suggest 'lazy'?) mental habits. This poor mental hygiene affects the other three in four of the population and if depression is a black dog, minor glumness is nothing more than a greyish spaniel. And to confuse my metaphors and adages, you can teach a grey spaniel new tricks.

The Tigger v Eeyore polarization hints at the fact that we all have a natural disposition. For example, Tigger might have a happiness range of 70–100, while Eeyore might range from 10–40. That means Tigger's range is somewhere between 'very happy' and 'insufferable' while Eeyore's top end only rises as far as 'not too bad, considering'.

Lampooning it as a cartoon merely reminds us of the happiness pie (from Boffin Island) in which we all have an in-built genetic baseline that is your happiness starting point. The good news is that whatever your current state of positivity or negativity, researchers have discovered that the ability of the brain to form new ways of thinking, lasts throughout our entire lives.

Yes, there is hope for us all.

Cultural Mediocrity

••••••

'IF YOU THINK ADVENTURE IS DANGEROUS, YOU SHOULD TRY ROUTINE. IT'S LETHAL.'

••••••

Paulo Coelho

Richard Dawkins introduced the idea of the meme, defined as 'an idea, behaviour or style that spreads from person to person within a culture'. Memes have become so well embedded that we stop challenging them and start becoming them![39]

For example, Australians call the Brits 'whinging Poms', tarring the entire nation with the glumness brush. And you don't have to listen too closely to detect an undercurrent of perpetual grumbling about just about anything and everything. We have been bathed in the familiarity of negativity to the point of it becoming ingrained in our culture, a phenomenon that is rather neatly observed in this satirical news item:

> *George Farthing, a British man living in America, was diagnosed as clinically depressed. He was tanked up on antidepressants and scheduled for a controversial shock*

therapy when doctors realized he wasn't depressed at all, he was just British.

Farthing, a man whose characteristic pessimism and gloomy perspective were interpreted as serious clinical depression, was led on a nightmare journey through the American psychiatric system. Dr Isaac Horney, a psychotherapist, explored Farthing's family history and couldn't believe his ears. Farthing spoke of growing up in a grey little town where it rained every day, of treeless streets lined with identical houses, and of passionately backing a football team that never won.

Identifying Farthing as British changed the diagnosis from 'clinical depression' to 'rather quaint and charming'. He was immediately discharged from the hospital with a selection of brightly coloured leaflets and an 'I ♥ New York' T-shirt.

Remember, as gregarious creatures, our instinct is to fit into cultural norms.

A very common mindset is to expect an average day and then if something good does come along, it's a bonus. You have probably never sat down and told yourself this was your strategy, it just seeped in as a way of thinking, another autopilot meme. Such a strategy will get you a whole load of average days with an occasional random corker, when something goes especially well. The safety net is, of course, that you will rarely be disappointed.

An alternative, somewhat riskier strategy might be 'maximizing' – otherwise known as 'going for it' – the very opposite of 'making do'. Maximizing involves setting your happiness sights very high, anticipating and expecting a fabulous day, deliberately looking out for the good stuff that might happen. The reason that this mindset is so rare is that it has no safety net. The risk is that the world will conspire to conjure a whole heap of dog mess and your expectation will be soiled so, yes, you might be disappointed.

I am not for the unbridled Pollyanna school of optimism. Not only is *Oooh, cancer. Thanks Doc. What a great opportunity to get a new wig* not very funny, it's also plain ridiculous. But a sense of what I call 'realistic optimism' will, I feel, massively increase your odds of having loads more amazing days. Realistic optimism reels you in from the Pollyanna end of the spectrum, but only by a bit. A new day really does herald a new dawn (one that you actually take a moment to notice) and it is up to you which attitude you select.

One of the 'problems' of choosing positives is that it goes against the grain of millions of years of human evolution. When we look around at our abundant lives, it's easy to forget that our ancestors eked out a meagre living. They lived in small groups. It was very uncommon for them to meet someone they didn't know and often dangerous when they did. Couple that with starvation, parasites, injury, no prescription drugs, no police – the world really was a dangerous place. The human brain was moulded by the need to survive and reproduce. It evolved with a hair-trigger readiness to react to danger. In fact, from a survival standpoint, if you failed to heed danger there would be no tomorrow.

For example, your great great great great great great great great great great grandpa could make two kinds of mistakes: first, thinking there was a snake in the bushes when there wasn't one, and second, thinking there was no snake in the bushes when there actually was one. The cost of the first mistake was a pounding heart and needless anxiety. The cost of the second one was death. Consequently, we evolved to make the first mistake a million times to avoid making the second one even once.

Cut to today and the dangers have receded but the same brain circuitry is continually scanning for danger. Indeed, Evan Gordon suggests that the brain scans the environment five times a second, looking for danger![40] This is just the way it is. It's not just you, it's the human race. Negativity bias is always lurking in the background.

Another manifestation of negativity bias is that you end up under-reacting to good stuff. The good stuff slips right through your attention, making little impact on your brain. While danger registers 9.8 on the Richter scale, shaking your worldly foundations, happiness whimpers in at .04

The result is that negativity bias tilts your world towards immediate survival, but away from happiness, peace, contentment and joy. It's why negative news gets reported and spread so much more readily. It's why we can't turn away from a car accident or two people fighting. It's why it's so much more tempting to relate to others through complaining and gossip rather than through gratitude. The media creates 'outrage porn', so rather than report on real stories, they find it more profitable to broadcast something offensive to create outrage, and then broadcast that outrage back across the population in a way that creates more outrage. So the news is not the news. The news is the protest/petition/fight/march/anger/outrage that the news has caused.

Stop and reflect, just for a second. How often do you yell at the TV news? Have you become addicted to being offended? In which case it's time to make a personal commitment to change your ways.[41]

When I was eight I had a beautiful yellow budgie called Sammy Dodger. My sis and I would close the windows in the lounge and let him out for a flutter. Except one day I forgot to close the window and Sammy escaped. We watched, open mouthed, as Sammy flew around the garden a couple of times, chirping with glee, not quite believing his luck and then, wham, he was bombarded by pigeons.

It seems Sammy wasn't such a dodger after all? He was grounded. I eventually found his body in a bush; he'd been pigeoned to death.

If you're a happy person who enjoys living life – here's some BREAKING NEWS – not everyone is like you. I think there might be a message in Sammy Dodger's story? Something like, 'Happy people, beware! All that vibrancy and colour? Standing out can be a risky strategy.'

We use the term 'mood hoover' to describe someone who's stuck in a rut of negativity. We're not talking about depression, more of a habitual low-level whinging. I call them 'mood hoovers' because they're expert at sucking all the positivity out of you, leaving you feeling exhausted too! I describe their outlook as 'every silver lining has a cloud!'

Negativity definition

He was such a mood hoover that even his blood group was negative.

Shonette calls them 'lemon suckers' and Andy W calls them 'happiness terrorists' – I don't think the vast majority mean to unleash their unhappiness warfare on unsuspecting family and friends. But they do have a canny knack of walking into a room and letting off a misery grenade or negativity bomb. Your cheery 'Good morning' is met with a stern-faced 'What's so good about it?' and BOOM! they've accidentally sucked all the happiness out of the room.

Let me be clear. They are not horrible people. Far from it. They are just tuned into negativity and have made it an art form. It's their natural wavelength. I once met a head teacher who confessed to having an 'infestation' of mood hoovers in her staffroom.

Postcard from a mood hoover

Currently staying in Yosemite and it would be great but the mountains are blocking all the views.

So, what on earth are we supposed to do about mood hoovers? We can't just give up on them, can we? Or ignore them? Or should we raise our effervescence to 'irritating level' in order to piss them off? And what if we've married one, or, heaven forbid, we are one?

> Definition of a mood hoover
>
> *Even his lucky break went gangrenous.*

Contrary to popular belief, the most unselfish thing you can do is be happy in your own skin because the best (some might say the only) way to inspire others to be happy and reach their full potential is to strive to be yourself, brilliantly. Some will follow and some won't. The problem is that some people, the really ingrained mood hoovers, seem to have been inoculated against your viral happiness. A bit like the MMR jab, they didn't just have one inoculation, they had the whole set and seem immune from ever catching mirth, merriment and rejoicing.

The irony is that they're the ones who need it the most. If you'd asked me a few years ago, I'd have given you some wishy-washy answer that was full of bull and bluster, as if there was some sort of social Tai Chi that you could practise on other people. The more mature version of me acknowledges the selfish angle to happiness. This book is about you. There is a kind of social Tai Chi, but you have to do it on yourself.

So, here are the three 'rules' for dealing with mood hoovers. Some may call them 'challenges' or 'self Tai Chi'.

Firstly, the adage 'if you can't beat 'em, join 'em', is way off the mark. When confronted by a mood hoover it's important that you don't get dragged down to their level. So you need a big dose of resilience in order to maintain your 'upbeatness', and it's not easy. It's a bit like when you're on an aeroplane, taxiing for take-off and the stewardess goes through the safety routine. 'If the cabin pressure falls, a mask will appear and,' she says, 'You must always put your own mask on first'. And my mind always questions this advice. *Isn't that a bit selfish? Should I not be helping my children with their oxygen masks first? Or the old lady in front of me?* The simple answer is... nope. Think of your happiness as your oxygen mask. The adage 'looking after number one' might be deemed selfish but in a positive psychology context, being happy is the least selfish thing you can do. It's only then you'll be in a position to help others.

Secondly, although you can't change mood hoovers, the open-looped nature of emotion means you can influence them. In fact, you cannot NOT influence them. Emotions are asymmetric, with the negative being more powerful and longer lasting than the positive. Schopenhauer sums it up as 'the weakness of wellbeing and happiness, in contrast to the strength of pain'. I think of positive emotions as carefree day trippers skipping along in a seaside town run by dictators of negativity who rule with an iron fist. So the skipping soon ceases. We remember bad service but delete good service. We remember the idiot who cuts us up in the traffic but conveniently delete all the excellent courteous drivers. That's why anxiety and depression can become chronic. They occupy the mind and convince it to gorge itself on a rich supply of negative thoughts.

So, change number three is to challenge yourself to be different. True, it didn't work for Sammy Dodger, but we're pretty sure it will work for you.

Provocative Therapy

A plan to make airports happier …

Recently, my passport application got rejected. Reason? My photo has the smallest inkling of a smile and, of course, you're not allowed to smile on your passport photo.

How about we turn that policy on its head so that you HAVE to smile on your passport photo. In fact, all applications will be rejected unless there's a big cheesy grin spread across your picture.

So, on entering a country, everyone would have to approach passport control and do their bestest grin. The passport holder would be happy and I'm sure immigration officers would feel uplifted too.
#genius

Happiness, like depression, is a self-reinforcing cycle. Happiness enhances volition, which in turn increases happiness, and away you go. Indeed, the greatest gift of happiness may not be in the feeling itself but rather in the accompanying thrill of possibility. Suddenly the world is in full surround sound HD 3D technicolour! The eye sees more clearly, the mind thinks more keenly, the heart beats faster and everything seems possible.

I love the work of Gretchen Rubin.[42] She weighs in to the 'money doesn't buy happiness' conundrum by suggesting that neither does good health. When money or health are problems, you think of little else. But when they're not a problem, you hardly think about them at all. In fact, you tend to take them for granted! Rubin isn't saying that good health and a pleasing bank balance aren't important – used wisely, each contributes massively to your overall life satisfaction. Once again, we're back to 'attention' as your conduit to happiness.

Therapy and counselling have mushroomed into some sort of 'grief ombudsmen' who you can turn to in troubled times. Happiness is so desirable that if we're not experiencing enough of it, we can get it prescribed.

To paraphrase Bono's assertion that 'Sunday Bloody Sunday' is not a rebel song, this section is not anti-medication. I appreciate that a swathe of the population has benefited from prescription meds and that they can ease whatever angst you may have. You are a walking talking cocktail of chemicals and if your mixture falls out of kilter then it can make sense to take something that balances you up again.

But let's take a peek at some facts. There's been a massive surge in psychiatric ill-health. At the beginning of the 20th century it was estimated that 1 in a 1000 people had some form of mental health problem. In the 1950s it had grown to 1 in 100 and today's widely quoted '1 in 4' statistic seems to be a genuine figure. As the UK population pushes towards 70 million citizens, that's a whopping 17.5 million people experiencing some sort of diagnosable mental disorder at any one time.

So, hang on, we've gone from 1 in 1000 to 1 in 4? Soon will it be abnormal to be normal? I'll be singled out as the weirdo who hasn't got a disorder. They'll be whispering about me in the office, 'Andy's not normal. I looked in his briefcase and guess what? No meds. What a freak.'

Of course, this whispering will make me feel insecure, thereby giving me some sort of paranoid disorder. Luckily, there are meds for that so, phew, I can begin to fit in with the crowd.

••••••
TAKING AN ANTIDEPRESSANT IS LIKE BURNING DOWN THE WHOLE FOREST BECAUSE ONE TREE IS DISEASED.
••••••

Ruby Wax

The *Diagnostic and Statistical Manual of Mental Disorders* (*DSM*) is the psychiatric bible that lists every conceivable mental illness known to human kind. The inaugural 1952 version listed 106 disorders and, with Freudian thinking dominating at the time, included homosexuality, ('pathological hidden fear of the opposite sex caused by traumatic parent–child relationships') which remained until draft 2 in 1974!

Yes, really!

Today's *DSM* (version 5) lists about 300 disorders; that's nearly three times as many disorders than in the 1950s.

It's estimated that 15 per cent of children now suffer from a diagnosable mental disorder.[43] As for adults, 26.2 per cent of American adults suffer from at least one of the *DSM* disorders in a given year with similar figures reported by the UK's ONS.[44] I haven't read all 947 pages but I'm told that *DSM5* includes bereavement as a major depressive disorder, so feelings of deep sadness, loss, sleeplessness, low appetite and crying – if they continue for more than two weeks after the death of a loved one – can be diagnosed as depression. Common sense suggests these are simply the natural part and parcel of experiencing a significant loss. Allen Frances suggests that 'Reclassifying bereavement as a symptom of depression will not only increase the rates of unnecessary medication but also reduces the sanctity of bereavement as a mammalian and human condition.' This substitution of a medical ritual for a much more important time-honoured one, is, according to Frances, another step in the wrong direction. Frances calls it 'diagnosis inflation',[45] or as James Davies suggests more chillingly than I could ever do, the increasing numbers of medicated people will become 'statistical droplets in the ever-expanding pool of the mentally unwell'.[46]

I don't generally subscribe to conspiracy theories but it's worth questioning the trustworthiness of the *DSM*: a list of disorders compiled by the same people who decreed homosexuality to be a disease and suggested masturbation leads to insanity. The same professionals who invented 'drapetomania' as a mental illness that caused black slaves to flee captivity, and who made kleptomania a disease rather than a motivated behaviour called 'stealing'. It's not the general population who are bonkers, it's the shrinks who have somehow invented a disorder for everything. I think that common sense, one day, will prevail, and we'll revise the *DSM* back to basics of real diseases. About a couple of dozen should do.

The mental health system teaches us to be shit scared of our own thoughts and to keep within the straight and narrow of conventional thinking. We tranquilize, calm and sedate those who go outside of normality. We medicate people to make them more manageable. Including children! Once decontaminated and 'under control' they can be released back into the wild.

Putting aside the double conspiracy of whether the pills actually work (check out James Davies' *Cracked* and make up your own mind) and the suspicion that naturally arises when the pharma industry sponsors the doctors who are conducting the trials (it's akin to Glaxo SmithKline sponsoring Lance Armstrong), the modern-day notion appears to be edging towards *there's no need to ever suffer emotionally because you can take a pill for it*. Whatever 'it' happens to be. Summing up, the medical view suggests that there is no value in suffering so we can swiftly curtail it through chemicals or therapy.

> Truth time
>
> *Pain is an inextricable thread in the fabric of life. To tear it out is not only impossible but destructive because everything else unravels too.*

So, let me elucidate on the polar opposite schools of thought as far as 'suffering' goes. The positive vision suggests that suffering has a redemptive role to play in life; in all instances there is something to be gained from suffering. In the midst of suffering, these aren't always obvious but a traumatic episode or the loss of a loved one can give you a new perspective or an inner strength. I could give dozens of examples from my research but I've narrowed it down to a couple of real quotes from real people:

'I lost a good friend a few years ago. It made me think about life. Thinking back, I guess it triggered some big changes for me.'

'Since the personal loss of my 11-year-old son. I don't take life for granted since then and try to enjoy every moment of my waking life.'

Please note, these quotes are from my flourishing group – happy within themselves and whom others are noticing as uplifting too. Excuse the lack of academia here but this is proof that shit really does happen. Both are powerful examples of the willingness to stare adversity in the face and shove your middle finger back at it.

I know there are multiple causes of mental suffering but what if most problems are created by the context in which people live and therefore require contextual not chemical solutions? As Breggin suggests, 'People who are breaking down are often like canaries in a mineshaft. They are the signal of a severe family issue.'[47]

So, rather than racing to a pharma solution, it might be worth trying to sort out the meaning or context, upgrade the thinking, prioritize relationships and/or enhance the environment.

There are some big thoughts in there somewhere.

Big thought number 1: Rather than, 'You've been made redundant? Here's a pill to ease your suffering', what if sadness, crying, anguish and misery are purposeful? What if they're designed into the human blueprint and, far from being a malady to be cured, emotional discontent is a state from which we learn and grow? Trauma builds resilience – so by taking your meds, you are alleviating (or at least numbing) the suffering but by-passing the anguish also means you by-pass the learning. So the next big catastrophe that happens in your life (and I guarantee they will keep on coming) means that, once again, you are unable to cope and you reach for the meds once again.

Big thought number 2: Following on, what if medicine is therefore trying to cure something that was never designed to be treated? Is it a coincidence that as life has accelerated and communities become more estranged, the various disorders have sky-rocketed? Is it a coincidence that as technology has exploded and we've gotten busy on social media, that we've mislaid the traditional systems of meaning that once kept us out of the grips of human despair?

Big thought number 3: What if this '1 in 4' phenomenon was caused by seismic societal shifts, a sort of grating of community tectonic plates. The Church, for so long the community crutch that gave focus, belief, purpose, comfort and rituals, is being subsumed underneath a secular society that has replaced God with mammon. So whereas religion had a neat way of explaining suffering, we now drown it out with purchases, busyness, alcohol and meds.

Summing these three thoughts up (and I'm just throwing this out there), what if mushrooming mental illness is not 'illness' in a medical sense? It's a natural by-product of struggling to find meaning and to keep up with the Joneses. We're driven to work and consume. It's not us malfunctioning, it's society and we have ended up seeking medical assistance for a non-medical problem.

••••••

'THE ONLY TRICK IN LIFE IS TO BE GRATEFUL FOR YOUR HIGHS AND GRACEFUL WITH YOUR LOWS.'

••••••

George Pransky

Please note, we are not suggesting we stop taking our meds or cancel our therapy appointment. For some, seeking professional help is necessary to get them on the right track. It is important to understand that simply having a positive mindset won't actually stop bad things from happening, but it does give you the tools to better deal with bad situations.

Sometimes your coping skills come down to nothing more than refusing to give in to your negative side and your fears.

Bedtime Story-Time...

I was reading a book to my two girls (Ellie is five 'well, I'm nearly six actually!', and Faye is four, 'but I'm a big girl too, aren't I Daddy!') before bedtime. It's called 'The Saddest King' and is about a kingdom where everyone was always happy and smiling.

Nobody ever cried, moaned or complained because the King had ordered everyone to 'always be happy'. Then one day a boy was upset because his dog had died, and he had loved his dog very much. When the King's guardsmen saw him crying, they took him to the King to explain why he was not being happy.

The King had a permanent smile on his face; it was the widest smile the boy had ever seen. When he told the King why he was upset and explained some of the good times he had shared with his dog (by this time the story was starting to get to my emotions too...!), he noticed that the King was also making sobbing noises. But strangely he still had a smile on his face.

At this point, the King pulled off his mask and revealed his true identity. He was crying openly. The King then explained that he too had once owned a pet dog who he had also loved very much, but who had also died. He was so upset that he had ordered everyone in the kingdom to always be happy, to take his mind off his feelings. He had then adopted the mask to hide his sorrow.

For years he had hidden his true emotions behind his mask, and everyone around him had also hidden their true feelings. When the word got round about the King being so upset, everyone else in the kingdom had a good cry – 'because they hadn't had a good cry in years'.

And I thought, what a lovely story about it being Okay to be sad.

(Email received from 'Art of Being Brilliant' delegate,
Paul Nutten)

What a beautifully crafted email. Of course, it's perfectly natural to feel sad. The problem arises when it's needless sadness that seeps into prolonged and insidious negativity. People can become so accustomed to negative thinking that their conscious mind will pull them down, even when they have done nothing wrong. These people become insecure, overly apologetic and indecisive. Worse still, they open the door to numerous stress-related problems.

In a perverse conspiracy of quantum physics, things that go wrong often make the best memories. A few years ago my family went on a holiday to Portugal. Lovely, sunny, hot Portugal. *Not!* One day it rained so hard that the streets flooded. There were lots of adults and seven kids in our party. On the third day of rain I decided to take the kids outside to do some 'rain bathing'. 'Get your swimmers on,' I challenged them, 'and let's get this holiday up and running.' Cue some quizzical looks and some gasps of exasperation from my mother-in-law as she pointed to the hammering rain.

Myself and the kids (aged 5 to 15) marched out, lay our towels on the sun loungers and spread ourselves out, in the pouring rain. Let me be clear, the rain was so hard that it hurt. Matt, aged seven, stretched out on his 'sun bed' and shouted in a posh English voice how much he adored rain bathing. James, aged five, started rubbing the rain into his skin, suncream style. It was proper hilarious and, for me, easily the highlight of the holiday.

Three years later at a family gathering, we asked the kids if they fancied going on another family holiday. James, now eight, piped up, 'Can we go rain bathing?' *#GoForIt*

Excavating Your Past

Let's get properly controversial: if therapy and medication worked, we wouldn't have the statistic of '1 in 4'. There is a great deal of excellent therapy and some awesome therapists but I ask you to use your common sense – is fixating on your problems and negative emotions going to make you feel better?

To bring up hurtful thoughts from past traumas, believing this will heal the pain, doesn't work for me on any level. Syd Banks nailed it when he said 'going back into the past is like going back into the shower to dry off'.

My dad has always been a DIY accident waiting to happen. His left thumb is twice the width of his right, simply because it's been hammered so many times. One of his classic near-death experiences involved failing to wear protective eye-wear which resulted in a chunk of metal becoming embedded in his eye. After a visit to accident and emergency, dad returned home with a huge bandage sellotaped across his eye. Obviously we fell about laughing but I imagine it hurt like hell.

In order for it to heal my dad didn't remove the bandage every night and reinsert the piece of metal, reliving the traumatic experience. Neither did he feel the need to meet up with other people who'd had similar DIY/gardening mishaps, reinserting screwdrivers into forearms and hammering their thumbs just to show everyone how painful their accidents were.

He left the wound well alone and, guess what, it healed itself. Plus, he used the whole painful episode as a learning experience. He has learned to be more careful and has invested in a pair of safety goggles.

Robert Holden reckons that anyone who reaches the ripe old age of 30 has enough reasons to be miserable for the remainder of their life. We all experience horrible things and end up feeling very low. The modern way is to seek medical advice for the low, in which case you will receive drugs or therapy, whereas for all but the very worst cases, the likelihood is that your mind will heal itself.

I love Ann Masten's concept of 'ordinary magic' – our in-built ability to be super-resilient.[48] This isn't for those trivial 'dog turd on the pavement of life' moments, this is for when you've fallen into a barrel of the stuff. Someone you love will die (this will happen several times in your life), or your relationship will break up (again, this might happen several times) or through no fault of your own, your job disappears or you get terribly ill (several times...) When there's a seismic event in your life, it can shake your foundations or it can reduce you to rubble.

You are a superhero, born with the power of self-healing. Ann Masten's concept of 'ordinary magic' means that emotions have the same healing power as your skin and bones. Providing your built-in resilience systems are in-tact, the chances are you'll be able to bounce back from almost anything. Your 'ordinary magic' will be more powerful if you've been fortunate enough to form secure relationships at an early age. It also helps if you have a brain that's in reasonable working order and it's a massive bonus if you're part of a community that is supportive and nurturing. In other words, resilience doesn't require anything rare or extraordinary, but instead requires that basic human adaptive systems are operating normally.

Thinking inside the box

Latin: *Semper in merda; sola altitudo variat*

Translation: *We're always in the shit, it's just the depth that varies*

Therefore, learning to bounce back is part of your in-built happiness mechanism. The aforementioned seismic events mean you will have happiness down-time but your set point acts to quake-proof your future. To continue the metaphor a little too far, you'll be severely shaken but not reduced to rubble.

Resilience isn't about instructing yourself to be positive or pretending the negative isn't there. Rather, it's more about being receptive to positives, noticing them and focusing your attention on them. So noticing that the sun is rising, this bread smells so crusty and fresh, the children are laughing, I'm breathing, look at the way the raindrops are running down the window pane, I'm in a supermarket (what an astounding choice of food), I have eyes, isn't it amazing to live in a society where someone turns up and takes my rubbish away, my skin is waterproof, I can read and write, I turn my cooker on and North Sea gas arrives (how the hell did that happen?) and suchlike.

Most people spend an inordinate amount of time focusing on what they haven't got. Happy people tend to be much more grateful for what they have got. Noticing these things focuses your attention. It won't guarantee happiness but gratitude acts like fertilizer for resilience.

A potentially scary thought.

We already know that owners look like their dogs, right? That's because on a subconscious basis, we choose mutts that are similar to us. Now, there's evidence to suggest that you may eventually grow to look like your partner. Couples who live together for decades tend to have had the same experiences and spend a lot of time in rapport. This matching of emotions on the inside creates facial features – frowns, wrinkles, laughter lines, whatever – that show up on the outside. Apparently your facial muscles will be sculpted by time to match those of your long-term partner, so facially, it pays to marry a smiler.

Top Tips

1. Rule #6: I love Ben Zander's 'rule number 6'[49] in which he recounts a story of an American President who was getting very serious and heavy in a meeting with the leader of a foreign nation. His aide approached him and said, 'Mr President Sir, please don't forget rule number 6'.

   The other head of state looked quizzically at the US President and, as you would, she inquired, 'What is rule number 6?'

And the President beamed and said, 'Rule number 6 is "don't take yourself too seriously".'

'And the other rules?'

The President's eyes were now twinkling. 'There aren't any,' he grinned. 'Just rule number 6.'

And, nice story as it is, it is also a good rule to live your life by. Sure, life can be a serious business and you've contracted this terrible disease called 'responsibility', but that doesn't mean you have to become deadly serious. A bit of levity helps you swallow the bitter aftertaste of some of life's more unsavoury moments.

2. Switch off your 'judge-ometer'. You know that nagging internal voice, the inner-critic that makes assumptions about everyone and everything, your judge-ometer that's set to 'snap judgement mode'? It's wearing you out. Switch it off. As psychology professor Ellen Langer says 'we are frequently in error but rarely in doubt'. Instead, take four seconds, in your head, to send warmth and love to everyone you meet.

3. Park your troubles (you can always come back to them if you miss them). An interviewer asked (scandal-ridden Olympic ice-skater) Tonya Harding how she could concentrate on her routine with gossip and bad news swirling around her. Harding's

answer? As she enters the rink, she picks a spot on the wall by the door, touches it with her finger, and pretends to store all her worries in that one spot. Then she skates with a clear mind, knowing she can resume her worrying when she leaves the rink.

4. (Advanced level) Dealing with negativity in other people ... The Japanese call it 'social *aikido*' ('the art of peace'). It's about neutralizing the mood hoover without causing them distress. You have three choices:

   i. Modify the social situation. Ask yourself, honestly, is there a way in which I might inadvertently be feeding this person's negativity? Might I be accidentally bating them?

   ii. Attend differently. In negative situations, most people tend to focus on what they're not getting (this person's not listening to me, this person's being unfair ...). It's a better tactic to focus on what you can give more of. Can I listen better? Can I give more warmth? Can I give more time or attention?

   iii. Change the meaning. Could this person be a teacher in disguise? It's a challenge for me not to get ground down. What can I learn about me?

Island of ENLIGHTENMENT
Life

Chapter 10

THE ISLAND OF ENLIGHTENMENT

● ● ● ● ● ●

In which we ask whether the same rules apply in Hunger Games and Happiness Games.

Oh, and on The Island of Enlightenment, fight club rules apply too.

We ask, 'What's new?' four times before coming to an answer. We learn that the neighbourhood's been on skid row for more than a century. Then it's off to check the view from Planet Zog before coming back to earth and learning from playtime in Leeds.

Of course, no personal development book is ever complete without The Muppets and MC Hammer. We plea for good Amazon reviews before likening happiness to Venice and then, with Lewis Carroll breathing down our necks, we manage to start a revolution and finish with the question, what have the Greeks ever given us? (apart from yoghurt, orgies and marbles. Oh, and Prince Philip).

This chapter marks the end of our happiness tour. In case we don't get a chance at the end, we'd like to take this opportunity to thank you for choosing to travel with us. It's been a ball!

••••••
CAFUNE (PORTUGUESE): TENDERLY RUNNING FINGERS THROUGH A LOVED ONE'S HAIR.
••••••

Hunger Games

Our hunch is that people who buy personal development books aren't actually the ones who really need them? Andy W. and I wrote a book boldly called *The Art of Being Brilliant* and I doubt very many neg-heads ever browsed the shelves, licking their lips in enthusiasm, thinking 'yep, that's the book for me.'

I've noticed that most people at the gym seem to be pretty fit already? They're going to the gym to remain fit. This is not some sycophantic nod to our readers. It's a very strong likelihood that you've bought this book to sharpen and hone your emotional fitness into the psychological equivalent of a happiness six-pack.

Another point worth noting is that you don't really want this book. In exactly the same way that when you buy a drill, you don't want a drill – you want holes. And you don't want a washing machine, you want clean clothes. You don't really want eight pints of beer, you want to feel good. As with everything else you spend your hard-earned money on, you don't want the product, you want the feeling that results

181

from it and since this book has 'happiness' in the title, we can hazard a guess at what you actually want more of.

Interesting thought

West Indian fast bowler Tino Best's answerphone message was, 'This is Tino Best speaking, the fastest bowler in the world. I can't take your call right now but I'll get back to you as soon as I've practised how to get faster.'

Paul McKenna is one of my heroes – completely cool in a totally uncool way, his unwavering confidence shining through in the title of his books. I was particularly taken with *I Can Make You Thin*, which I bought and devoured (obviously, not literally, otherwise his book would have had the opposite effect).

I can make you thin? I considered my recent trip to buy some new jeans and being saddened by thrashing around in the changing room and catching sight of my rear end in the magic arse-magnifying mirror. Paul wasn't promising *I might be able to help you slim down a little bit* or even *I can make you less fat*. Nope, his bold claim was that he would make me thin.

It's a great book, padded a little, but all-in-all an enjoyable read. It's padded because this is basically it: On your hunger scale of 1 to 10, always eat when you reach a 3 or 4 (so never get reaaaally hungry) and stop eating when you're at a 7 or 8 (so don't stuff your face).

So scoff whatever you want but 'eat when you're hungry' and 'stop eating before you're full'. It's deliciously simple.

But so is food. And as simple as it may seem and as much as I know it makes perfect sense, *stop eating just before you're full* goes against everything I've ever been taught. In our house, the general rule is that you stop eating when it hurts and, even then, your pudding pipe will need filling (it's a separate tube you see, so no matter how much main course you have, you can always fit a pudding in).

If I ever dared leave anything, my mum used to remind me of the *starving children in Africa*, as if that fish finger was going to be air-freighted to Addis Ababa.

A few months after reading Paul's book I read a scathing 1* Amazon review, written by an angry reader, for whom the book hadn't worked. She had vented her spleen, good and proper. Another Amazon customer had then replied to her rant asking simply, 'Did you do what he said?'

And she replied a rather sheepish, 'Well, no, not really...' before listing a whole load of excuses.

Eat when you're hungry and *stop eating before you're full*. It seems that the 'game of hunger' is common sense that only works if you do it.

Ditto, 'happiness games'.

What's New?

Is anything new?

Over the centuries there have been huge socioeconomic changes that have swept through societies. Population growth, urbanization and the development of a transport infrastructure have had a profound effect on who we meet, do business with, go to school with and fall in love with. The last 200 years has seen the population explode from less than 1 billion to greater than 7 billion. More than half of that increase has been since 1960. As the population has shot up, so has mobility.

Tom Standage makes the point that, in the pre-telegraph USA, news travelled by foot or horse. Indeed, the 'Pony Express' was the fastest and most expensive way of getting something delivered.[50] The telegraph poles collapsed distance and time, putting the horses and riders out of work. Then came the telephone, initially treated with caution because the fear that listening to speech without seeing the person might be socially dangerous.

Charles Horton Cooley was a man ahead of his time; this quote from 1912 refers to the advent of the telephone: 'In our own life, the intimacy of the neighbourhood has been broken up by the growth of an intricate mesh of wider contacts which leaves us strangers to people who live in the same house... diminishing our economic and spiritual community.'[51]

Goodness me, this 'social media' thing isn't some passing fad, the neighbourhood's been on the slippery slope for more than 100 years.

So, I ask again, is anything actually new? The mantra of most personal development books is that a better life is waiting for you. It's somewhere over there. It's a mightily scary thought but what if nothing is waiting for you? Sure, you're probably doing the right thing and working your backside off, saving some money in a pension pot, so that magical retirement is yours for the taking. We're not saying jack it all in, buy a camper van and live every day as if it's your last. Ours has been a plea to enjoy every single day; in fact, squeezing the maximum happiness out of every single minute of every single day, seems like a worthwhile cause. This guide has been a double whammy of good news. Whammy one, there is a better life. And whammy two, it's not waiting for you. It's here. Now!

So, if that's not new, what is?

You learn to play by the 'happiness rules' and the result is that you experience short bursts of happiness and positivity. We have encouraged you to break the rules but it's a bit like fight club. The first rule of happy club is that you don't talk about happy club. You apply it. People don't want you blabbing on about how happy you are – they want to feel good in your presence and that means you live it. Breathe it maybe. If you're a living breathing example of an outstanding human being, you really don't need to be saying very much at all.

In terms of its transferability, we've argued that happiness is your moral duty. It's great for your health and wellbeing but it's also crucial life-blood for those around you. But 'moral duty' sounds rather heavy, and you don't need that responsibility. Plus, you already knew that?

So, we'll ask one more time, *is anything actually new?*

In order to make a significant dent in the universe, to create a positive ripple that is felt beyond immediate family and friends, there is one thing that needs to be new.

You.

Tectonic Plates

Looking from Planet Zog, our planet is as it is. It's been here a long time. Fingers crossed, it will continue to spin on its axis and, if we can take a bit more care with it, will sustain a breathable atmosphere for a good while yet. Earth does change, its plates shifting ever so slightly now and again as it gradually cools. Sloooooowly.

Life on earth evolves a tiny bit faster, but not so fast that you can see it. In your lifetime, monkeys will remain as monkeys and that blobfish will continue to blob.

Society got off to a slow start but, in recent times, has cranked change up to an eye-wateringly rapid pace. There are significant social changes that you will notice in your lifetime.

You, on the other hand, can change instantly. But only if you need to and, even then, only if you can be bothered. If the first rule of happy club is *don't talk about happy club*, the second rule might be *you have to be committed to happy club*.

Speaking of commitment, I did a two-day event at a school in the north of England. I was working with year 6s (age 10) and, at break time, I did what was expected of me – I sat in the staffroom, drank instant coffee and made small talk, while outside, 250 children buzzed around in a swarm of excitement, energy and giddy glee. I watched two little girls in particular. One was twirling around while the other guided her across the length of the playground. They had to stop for a minute while a game of football went on around them, and then they continued, the game seemed to be *how many twirls does it take to get from one end to the other?*. It looked rather fabulous and, to be honest, I was curious. But before they had finished, the bell went, the teachers slurped the last dregs, the twirling stopped, the bees lined up and everyone buzzed back to class.

I hatched a plot. Next day, same school and same kids. Feeling a little devilish, I announced to the kids that we were going to take over the staffroom and send the teachers out for break. 'You can't do that!' they said.

'Watch me!' At break time I'd arranged things so that years 5 and 6 were in the staffroom, while 23 adults were assembled for 'playtime' in the playground. The atmosphere in the staffroom was something I'd never experienced before: 75 children getting high on black coffee and ginger-snaps. It took me a while to get their attention and, when I did, I said, 'Guys, come over to the window and tell me what you see.'

Seventy-five pairs of eyes rested on 23 adults, standing awkwardly in the playground. There was no laughter, no running, no tig, no stuck in the mud and absolutely no *how many twirls does it take to get across the playground?*

The children wore genuine looks of perplexity. 'Why aren't they playing?' asked Jessica.

'Jess,' I said, 'I think they've just forgotten?'

••••••

'BEGIN AT THE BEGINNING,' THE KING SAID GRAVELY, 'AND GO ON TILL YOU COME TO THE END, THEN STOP.'

••••••

Lewis Carroll, Alice in Wonderland

We can't take you much further than the playground story. If you haven't got it by now, you probably never will. There's almost nothing new that you can say about happiness, because happiness isn't new. The playground story acts as a sharp reminder that this entire book hasn't been about 'personal development', it's been about 'personal remembering'.

The final leg of our epic happiness journey, has done what we said it would always do, bring you back home. We're hoping 'same place, different you'? All along we've been trying to avoid suggesting that *happiness is a journey rather than a destination*, because that cliché is well meaning but not true.

Happiness is both.

Happiness is most certainly a journey, but it's also a place you can settle into. You can literally build your foundations in happiness rather than living in the suburbs and travelling in on the bus. If happiness was a city, it would be Venice – too many day-trippers!

I Hear Ticking?

As Brené Brown says, with regards to life itself, 'Be in the arena!'[52] And if life truly is the ultimate arena a lot of cheap seats are taken by people who never venture onto the stage. It's easy to sit there, hurling insults, like Waldorf and Statler off *The Muppets*, but without the humour.

Statler: This show is awful.

Waldorf: Terrible!

Statler: Disgusting!

Waldorf: See you next week!

Statler: Of course.

We set out to write a book that is crammed with content but disguised in such a way that the reader would think it was just a whimsical travelogue through a few mystical lands. We get that it's not everyone's cuppa. To highlight our imperfections, we'd like to share an abominable Amazon review for one of our other books. The review, snappily titled, 'Pop psychology for (by) morons', reads thus: 'It is possible to dumb a subject down to the point where the text has no value whatsoever. This book achieves that "brilliantly", at the same time presenting its authors as trite and exploitative.'

It could have been written by Statler. Or Waldorf? Andy W was so upset at the injustice that he wanted to use it as an excuse to don his balaclava and 'beat some happiness into them'. On reflection, not only would that not work, but we agreed it's not quite in tune with the ethos of happiness. Instead, we decided to carry on doing what we do in the only way we know. Throwing soft fruit from the sidelines is all well and good, but the ones who add real value are in the arena, giving it a go.

We are particularly fond of this final land, The Island of Enlightenment. It's a wonderful place to live because it's entirely constructed in your head. Your outside world might be Zombie Land, Money Mountain or The Forest of Negativity but inside, you are enlightened. It's a great place to leave you.

It has been an exacting journey so thanks for staying with us. From here, you are able to take the learning from all of the other lands and see how they fit together. We figure that you can work it out for yourself? When you do, you'll notice the shift to healthy functioning is contagious. It attracts and engages others. Some people are 'naturals' in their positive outlook, others might require a bit of extra help, but we're all capable of it. However, the more I learn the less inclined I am to suggest that we need to take responsibility for other people's happiness?

It's quite empowering to realize that we don't have to carry that burden. We can't 'fix' other people. Regarding happiness, you can adopt the strategy of 'safety in numbers'. That basically means that you wait for everyone else to be happy and then join in. This strategy is flawed in that you'll probably die waiting. Or you can quit waiting for the happiness revolution and create one.

Happiness is one of the few times when I'd encourage you to be totally selfish. It's all about you. The underlying theme of the happiness landscape is that all you can do is take charge of your own thoughts and let your best self shine.

Your happiness lesson is you.

But when? That's not quite as stupid as it might sound. I once had a delegate suggest that he didn't have time to be happy, so he was going to schedule it in for 'about November time' (the course took place in March!) And, no, he wasn't being ironic or facetious, he explained that he had a lot on at work but 'things will have quietened down by about November'. I'm not sure how much you can miss a point by?

There are lots of versions of time and we all have our personal favourites – mine are 'dinner time', 'bedtime', 'quiet time', 'me-time' and 'down-time'. My all-time #1 is 'family-time'.

MC Hammer had a very special version of time that he so vocally reminded us, couldn't be touched. Whilst MC Hammer rapped a good lyric and danced a decent baggy-trousered dance, his concept of 'Hammertime' made no sense whatsoever.

The Greeks on the other hand? They have two versions of time. *Chronos* is the time that you and I think of, the ticking *Countdown* clock variety. The time of day, the stage of life you're at – the point being that it's finite – when it's gone it's gone.

The Greeks also have *kairos*, a deeply personal sense of time. A realization that the time is right.

Chronos tells us that time is limited and *kairos* that the time is right. *Carpe Diem* ('seize the day') is therefore half right. We think you're better off seizing the moment.

Our entire book has been pointing to this very moment. Before the blob consumes us and we disappear back into the big ball of energy, it's '*kairos* time'. The time is right. Indeed, it always has been and it always will be.

Thank you for travelling with us. We never said it would be easy, but we promised you it'd be worth it.

Please check you've got all your belongings. Be careful when collecting your thoughts because they may have shifted during the trip.

We wish you a safe onward journey xxx

• • • • • •

WE THREE

There's larger than life, and there's Shonette Bason. Shonette is a freak of nature. A cross between Marilyn Monroe and Jessica Rabbit, Shonette experiences chronic happiness and is mad keen to share her enthusiasm for all things positive and uplifting. Shonette delivers keynotes and workshops to anyone who will listen. Mother of four, Man Utd fan, Guinness World Record Holder, hailing from a tiny community in the north east of England, Shonette also happens to be proper funny.

@shonettebason

www.spreadthehappiness.co.uk

Having somehow managed to leave school with next to nothing, Andy Whittaker has thrown himself into the art and science of positive psychology. Graduating from the university of life, Andy has done a variety of proper jobs (paper-round, army, holiday rep and sales) before finally landing his dream one – delivering a host of uplifting keynotes to adults and children. Originally from Morecambe (voted the third-worst place to live in the country) he now lives in Mansfield (recently voted the second-worst place to live). For obvious reasons, Andy's dream is to eventually retire to Hull.

@artofbrillandyw

www.artofbrilliance.co.uk

Derby born and bred, Andy Cope is a best-selling children's author who has also managed to stretch his PhD research to a full 12 years. Poking about in the lives of happy people and finding out why they're so happy – is that actually a job? He's not sure. But out of the theory comes a whole raft of simple happiness lessons which Andy now delivers in businesses and schools across the world.

Andy has also written several personal development books for adults and young people. He reckons he's got a massive book left in him – a game-changer that will revolutionize mind, thought and consciousness. It might even solve the Israeli/Middle East spat. He really hopes the ideas crystallize and the book makes it onto his laptop before he dies.

@beingbrilliant
www.artofbrilliance.co.uk

· · · · · ·

RECOMMENDED BOOKS AND MOVIES

Books

Andy Cope and Andy Whittaker, *Be Brilliant Everyday* (Capstone, 2014). Recommending your own back catalogue? How terribly shallow. Personal development from a refreshingly British perspective. Says it how it is. No bull.

Paul McGee, *SUMO (Shut Up Move On)* (10th edition, Capstone, 2015). Simple, humorous and a fabulous starting point. Highly recommended.

Daniel Goleman, *The New Leaders* (Golman, Boyatsiz & McKee, 2002). The guru of emotional intelligence finally writes a book that we can all understand.

David Taylor, *The Naked Leader* (Bantam, 2003). Leadership stripped of the big words and confusing jargon. Love it.

Richard Wiseman, *Quirkology* (Pan Books, 2007). Wiseman can do no wrong. Take it on your hols. Great website too.

Andy Cope, *The Little Book of Emotional Intelligence* (John Murray Learning, 2016). Andy is at pains to point out that the title is misleading – the book is neither 'little' nor about 'emotional intelligence'. It is however a book.

Dale Carnegie, *How to Win Friends and Influence People* (Vermillion, 2006). A classic, written decades ago but proof that human habits don't change. We all want to be liked. This gives you some clues so you can up your likeability factor.

Edward Monkton, *The Pig of Happiness* (HarperCollins, 2011). Takes one minute to read. Simple, obvious, enlightening and brilliant. Read it in the bathroom.

Victor Frankl, *Man's Search for Meaning* (Ebury Digital, 2013). Moving, scary, challenging and very sad. Ground breaking stuff from someone who survived a concentration camp. He did so because he refused to let the guards take away his spirit. And we thought we had problems!

Jamie Smart, *Clarity* (Capstone, 2013). Jamie has a knack of explaining complex issues very simply.

Robert Holden. *Success Intelligence* (Hay House, 2010). Completely brilliant. Spiritual undertones which would normally put me off, but Robert is such a wordsmith that he managed to take me with him. 'If God had one thought for you today, what would it be?' Shit, that's an awesome question, even if you're not religious!

Ben and Ros Zander, *The Art of Possibility* (Harvard Business School Press, 2000). Quirky and mad ... the Zanders have teamed up to write something completely original and very readable. It has a musical theme (Ben is a famous conductor) and some of the stories are first class.

Paulo Coelho, *The Alchemist* (HarperCollins, 1995). Read it and liked it. Then thought about it and wasn't sure I understood it. I think I need to read it again. Young lad goes off into the desert in search of meaning...lots of metaphors along the way. Good one for reading by the pool.

Danny Wallace, *The Yes Man* (Ebury Press, 2006). Completely brilliant as an entertaining thought-provoker. Danny uses a little poetic licence as he guides us through a six-month period where he said 'yes' to everything. Life changing indeed! And very funny!

Shawn Achor, *The Happiness Advantage* (Virgin Books, 2011). Lots of heavy academia distilled into plain common sense.

Simon Sinek, *Start with Why* (Penguin, 2011). Is the book as good as the TED talk? You decide.

Ruby Wax, *Sane New World* (Hodder & Stoughton, 2014). A luscious mix of cognitive behavioural therapy and pure comedy. Hard to beat.

Syd Banks, *Second Chance* (Fawcett, 1987). Pretty dire in terms of style, but a great insight into Syd's thinking.

Jack Pransky, *Somebody Should Have Told Us* (CCB Publishing, 2011). A much better account of Syd's work (see above) than Syd ever managed. Ditto Pransky's *Paradigm Shift*.

James Davies, *Cracked* (Icon Books, 2014). The truth behind the pharma industry. Scary stuff.

John Naish, *Enough* (Hodder & Stoughton, 2009). What if the secret to happiness wasn't starting new things but knowing when to stop? Naish is a genius.

Oliver Burkeman, *The Antidote* (Canongate Books, 2013). We reserve a special place in our hearts for people who rubbish what we do. And nobody does that better than Mr B.

Michael Bungay-Stanier, *The Coaching Habit* (Box of Crayons, 2016). A no-nonsense gem. Most coaches swear by the classic GROW model. I'd swear by this instead.

Movies

Want to learn but can't be bothered to read a book? Snuggle up on the sofa and press 'play':

It's a Wonderful Life (1946). Has all the attributes of a black and white oldie...awful acting, rubbish directing, cringeworthy dialogue...but the messages are spot on. Recently voted the best feelgood film of all time...

Pay it Forward (2000) ...but this one takes my vote. A brilliant movie based on the premise of random acts of kindness

The Shawshank Redemption (1994). Understand your impact as well as the power of remaining positive. A classic!

About Time (2013). The best Richard Curtis film, by a country mile. If you could revisit your past, which bit would you seek out and why? #OMG!

Toy Story 2 (1999). Woody is kidnapped but his friends rally round. Realization of the importance of being your authentic self.

Monsters Inc. (2001). Mike and Sully turn nightmares into laughter. Best 'business documentary' ever?

School of Rock (2003). Play to your strengths. Oh, and energy/enthusiasm are infectious!

How the Grinch Saved Christmas (2000). Green, ugly, hairy self-confessed grouch goes through some serious personal change!

Dead Poets Society (1989). *Carpe Diem*! Nuff said!

Groundhog Day (1993). Stuck in a way of thinking? Change your habits, change your life!

Kung Fu Panda (2008). There's no 'secret ingredient' in the soup! OMG! Is this a con or is it all about self-belief?

Life is Beautiful (1997). Completely brilliant – and I never thought I would say that about an Italian film dubbed into English. You absolutely must see this movie!

Untouchable (2012). French film (no, not that sort!) that has one of the best examples of emotional contagion ever. I'll let you pick him out. Yes, he's a bit naughty and rather un-pc, but what a difference he makes to the lives of the people around him. Feel the energy!

'Art of Being Brilliant': The Movie Just kiddin' (for now!)

NOTES

Chapter 2

1 Jamie Smart, *Clarity: Clear Mind, Better Performance, Bigger Results* (John Wiley & Sons, 2013)

2 Robert Holden, *Shift Happens* (Hay House, Inc., 2000)

3 Guy Browning, *Never Hit a Jellyfish With a Spade* (Gotham Books, 2004)

4 Anthony Seldon, *Beyond Happiness* (Hodder & Stoughton, 2015)

Chapter 4

5 Jamie Smart, *Clarity: Clear Mind, Better Performance, Bigger Results* (Capstone, 2013)

6 http://www.cityandguilds.com/news/November-2012/careers-happiness-index-2012#.WPSOcojytnl (accessed 2017)

7 https://www.thetimes.co.uk/article/you-cant-prosper-just-by-getting-richer-q0xcn592p (accessed 2017)

8 https://www.forbes.com/sites/learnvest/2012/04/24/the-salary-that-will-make-you-happy-hint-its-less-than-75000/#7822d2683247 (accessed 2017)

9 World Happiness Report 2017, http://worldhappiness.report/wp-content/uploads/sites/2/2017/03/HR17.pdf (accessed 2017)

10 Adam Galinsky and Maurice Schweitzer, *Friend & Foe: When to Cooperate, When to Compete, and How to Succeed at Both* (Crown Publishing Group, 2015)

11 Nattavudh Powdthavee. 'Putting a Price Tag on Friends, Relatives, and Neighbours: Using Surveys of Life Satisfaction to Value Social Relationships', Institute of Education, University of London: 13 April 2007

12 Jamie Smart, *Clarity: Clear Mind, Better Performance, Bigger Results* (Capstone, 2013)

13 Ruby Wax, *A Mindfulness Guide for the Frazzled* (Penguin Life, 2016)

14 John Naish, *Enough* (Hodder & Stoughton, 2008)

15 Robert Holden, *Success Intelligence* (Hay House, Inc. 2005)

16 Larry Dossey, *Space, Time and Medicine* (Boston, MA: Shambhala Publications, 1982), pp. 50–51.

17 Eckhart Tolle, *The Power of Now: A Guide to Spiritual Enlightenment* (Namaste Publishing, 1999)

18 James Wallman, *Stuffocation: Living More with Less* (Random House Publishing Group, 2015)

19 Chris Barez-Brown, *Free: Love Your Work, Love Your Life* (Penguin Group, 2014)

20 Michael Foley, *The Age of Absurdity: Why Modern Life Makes it Hard to be Happy* (Simon and Schuster, 2010)

21 Robert Holden, *Be Happy* (Hay House, Inc. 2009)

22 David Pollay, *The Law of the Garbage Truck* (Sterling, 2010)

23 John Naish, *Enough* (Hodder & Stoughton, 2008)

24 Dr Miguel Farias and Catherine Wikholm, *The Buddha Pill: Can Meditation Change You?* (Watkins, 2015)

25 Alain de Botton, *Status Anxiety* (Penguin, 2005)

Chapter 6

26 Sonia Lyubomirsky, *The How of Happiness: A Practical Guide to Getting the Life you Want* (Piatkus, 2010)

27 'Getting dirty may lift your mood', http://www.bristol.ac.uk/news/2007/5384.html (accessed 2017)

28 'Getting dirty may lift your mood', http://www.bristol.ac.uk/news/2007/5384.html (accessed 2017)

29 Martin Seligman, *Learned Optimism: How to Change Your Mind and Your Life* (Vintage, 2006)

30 Acacia Parks, quoted in Jarden, A., 'Positive Psychologists on Positive Psychology: Acacia Parks', *International Journal of Wellbeing*, (2012) 2(2), 98–104. doi: 10.5502/ijw.v2i2.7

31 Herbert Simon, as reported in *The Economist,* http://media.rickhanson.net/home/files/papers/ChoosingHappiness.pdf (accessed 2017)

Chapter 7

32 David Snowdon, *Ageing with Grace: What the Nun Study Teaches Us About Leading Longer, Healthier, and More Meaningful Lives* (Random House Publishing Group, 2008)

33 Steven Pinker, *How the Mind Works* (Penguin, 2003)

Chapter 8

34 Stanley Milgram, *Obedience to Authority: An Experimental View* (Tavistock Publications, 1974)

35 Garret Kramer, *Stillpower: Excellence with Ease in Sport and Life* (Astria Books, 2011)

36 David Eagleman, *The Brain: The Story of You* (Canongate Books, 2015)

37 Richard Wilkins: check him out at http://www.theministryofinspiration.com/

38 As reported in *The Telegraph*, http://www.telegraph.co.uk/news/health/news/12153001/58-million-anti-depressants-issued-every-year-equivalent-of-one-per-person-in-England.html (accessed 2017)

39 Richard Dawkins, *The Selfish Gene* (Oxford University Press, 1986)

40 Evian Gordon, *The Brain Revolution* (Dog Ear Publishing, 2016)

41 Oh, and by the way, it's worth considering that just because you're offended doesn't mean you're right!

42 Gretchen Rubin, *Better than Before: Mastering the Habits of Our Everyday Lives* (Two Roads, 2015)

43 Reported in James Davies, *Cracked: Why Psychiatry is Doing More Harm Than Good* (Icon Books, 2014)

44 http://www.depression-understood.org/information/othart2.htm (acccessed 2017)

45 Allen Frances lecture on the over-diagnosis of mental illness, available on YouTube: https://www.youtube.com/watch?v=yuCwVnzSjWA (accessed 2017)

46 James Davies, *Cracked: Why Psychiatry is Doing More Harm Than Good* (Icon Books, 2014)

47 Ann Masten, *Ordinary Magic: Resilience in Development* (The Guildford Press, 2014)

48 Ann Masten, *Ordinary Magic: Resilience in Development* (The Guildford Press, 2014)

49 Rosamund Stone Zander and Benjamin Zander, *The Art of Possibility* (Harvard Business School Press, 2000)

Chapter 10

50 Tom Standage, *The Victorian Internet: The Remarkable Story of the Telegraph and the Nineteenth Century's On-line Pioneers* (Walker & Co, 1998)

51 Charles Horton Cooley, *Social Organization: A Study of the Larger Mind* (Transaction Publishers, 1983)

52 Brené Brown, *Daring Greatly: How the Courage to Be Vulnerable Transforms the Way We Live, Love, Parent and Lead* (Penguin Group, 2012)

••••••

FOUR SPARE PAGES FOR THE ARTISTICALLY MINDED

Seeing as adult colouring books are in vogue, why not grab a pencil and draw what happiness means to you ...